Library of
Davidson College

Makeup for the Dark Complexioned Actor

by

Bessie G. Smith

and

George C. Brian

ORACLE PRESS

© 1983 By Oracle Press for the authors

Library of Congress No. 82–62535

ISBN No. 0–88127–012–1

Published in 1983 by
Oracle Press, Ltd.
All rights reserved.

Printed and Bound
by Land and Land Printers, Inc.
Baton Rouge, LA

Dedication

To Alfred and to Freida

TABLE OF CONTENTS

PREFACE: Why Study Makeup for the
    Dark Complexioned Person? v

CHAPTER I: Problems in Making Up the
    Dark Skinned Person 1

CHAPTER II: Principles Governing the Use of Makeup 7

CHAPTER III: The Youthful Look 13

CHAPTER IV: Middle and Old Age Makeup 23

CHAPTER V: Character and Racial Makeup 37

GLOSSARY 49

APPENDIX 53

PREFACE

WHY STUDY MAKEUP FOR THE DARK COMPLEXIONED PERSON?

"Makeup is for everyone and everyone can be made up."
— B. Grossley Smith

In decades past, the study of makeup was usually a pre-requisite or required course for a theatre or drama major. Over a span of years it has been brought into clearer focus and is now given the right to function as a separate, well-defined discipline of its own. It possesses as many diversified areas as any other discipline of the times. The field of makeup is of greater magnitude than most laymen would expect. Makeup no longer serves as a mere course of study; it is presently accepted as a true art form and a challenging vocation. It affords one a real adventure, allowing one's creativity to be used to the fullest. Within its parameters there is much room for experimentation and professional achievements. In spite of all this, little has been done in makeup for the dark complexioned actor.

This book is especially concerned with the problems surrounding stage makeup for the dark complexioned or black actor. It will be helpful to the makeup teacher and student, the makeup artist, and the non-professional person who desires to know more about how to apply theatrical makeup to this special group of people. We suggest simple but sound methods for solving problems incurred in making up the darkly pigmented actor. This book also features principles that govern the application of makeup as it appears on stage under various shades of lighting. We further discuss straight makeup, middle and old age makeup, and character makeup. We also look at several types of racial transformations.

Throughout this book there are photographs, drawings, and charts. There are a detailed glossary and an appendix to aid the reader's understanding.

Today, the role of the makeup artist in the professional as well as in the nonprofessional theatre demands great skill, for he is dealing with actors and actresses of more varied ethnic backgrounds than ever before. He must meet the continuing demands placed before him and conquer new challenges facing him. One of these challenges is make-up for the black or dark complexioned performer.

In a letter to the authors of this book, Dr. Floyd L. Sandle, formerly head of the Department of Speech at Grambling State University and later associated with Dillard University, had the following to say:

> I do feel that some specific work of this nature is needed and will probably be needed in as much as the future for black actors is likely to show more and greater improvement.
>
> For one thing there is likely to be more opportunities for black actors in the educational theatres as well as in the commercial theatres; on television and the like. Obviously, since there are black medical doctors and dentists, black college and university professors, black teachers in general, black nurses, black clerks in stores, and blacks in all phases of life, these characters will be believable on stage. There is or there will be a greater need to do creditable makeup jobs on these characters. For a black actor cannot make it on the stage without makeup any more than the white actor can. Thus, there is considerable merit in your concern with the problem.

The authors would like to thank the following individuals for their assistance during the writing of this book:

Thomas Bunch, Technical Director of Theatre at Northeast Louisiana University.
Harriet Cale, Sandel Library Archives at Northeast Louisiana University.
Cora DeBurr, Instructor of Speech and Drama at Ouachita High School.
Eddie Douzart, Mortician in Monroe, Louisiana.
Cindy Jeansonne, Photographer in Monroe, Louisiana.
Earl James Johnson, student at Northeast Louisiana University.
Prentiss Love, Director of Counseling and Testing Center at Grambling State University.
Vicky McDonald, Secretary for the College of Liberal Arts at Northeast Louisiana University.
William R. Rambin, Head of the Department of Communication Arts at Northeast Louisiana University.
John A. Sampognaro, Registered Pharmacist in Monroe, Louisiana.
Floyd L. Sandle, Division of the Humanities, Dillard University, New Orleans, Louisiana.
Allen Williams, Head of the Speech Department of Grambling State University.

CHAPTER I

PROBLEMS IN MAKING UP THE DARK SKINNED PERSON

Makeup is like painting a portrait, but with the dark complexioned person one begins with a black canvas.

— George Brian

The black actor will have less place in a regular make-up class designed specifically for the white person than individuals of other races. This is mainly because there is a wide difference between the coloring of the black and white student. Part of the problem is that almost no standard makeup company places any particular emphasis on products for the black actor. Artists have had to lean primarily on standard makeup for actors in general. Since the complexions of black actors are so diverse the standard makeup has usually been adequate.

There is no effective way to meet and satisfy the needs of the black students in a white oriented course unless the instructor is able to include knowledge about makeup for the person with dark skin. It is important that we as stage makeup artists and teachers possess some insight into the problems which could occur from ignoring the black person as a stage performer.

Normally we type people, and this should not be done in the realm of makeup for the black individual. We tend to categorize and group blacks according to their physical or biological characteristics. This cannot be done. There are skin tones too numerous to define or classify, ranging from black to shades of brown, tan, olive, to nearly white. Much racial intermixing has occurred over the centuries. In the past we have stereotyped black physical characteristics by their national origins. That is to say, we have assigned blacks prominent foreheads, low hairlines, thick eyebrows and almost bridgeless noses, wide flared nostrils, eyes spaced far apart, round to oval faces, accented with thick, prominently rimmed lips, no cheeks, and round chins. Above all they were very *black* with kinky hair.

Today, in selecting players for black families, in which the mother is light and the father is dark, the children may be either light or dark. Because of the biological arrangement, casting is sometimes a problem where acting talent is concerned. If both parents are light or dark complexioned the skin tones of the children should be matched to them. If the skin tones of the family are inappropriately matched, such as two light parents with a dark child or two dark parents with a light child, then one or both of the light parents should be darkened with make-up or the light child darkened.

Another consideration is the actor's skin. It must be kept in mind that darker complexions have porous skin which produces more oil; therefore, the skin must be properly prepared to a very dry condition prior to makeup application. During a performance, frequent check-up and touch-up sessions could be necessary. The skin seems to absorb the paint under the warm lights. Appendages such as crepe hair, nose putty and derma wax might have trouble staying on.

The ideal contour of the face is egg-shaped or nearly oval with the chin and jaw slightly narrower than the forehead. Many faces present a problem to straight makeup because they are not perfectly shaped. The round face, the square face, the oblong face, the cone-shaped face, and the diamond shaped face can be made to look more pleasing by the addition of moist rouge or lowlight colors to the appropriate parts of the face.

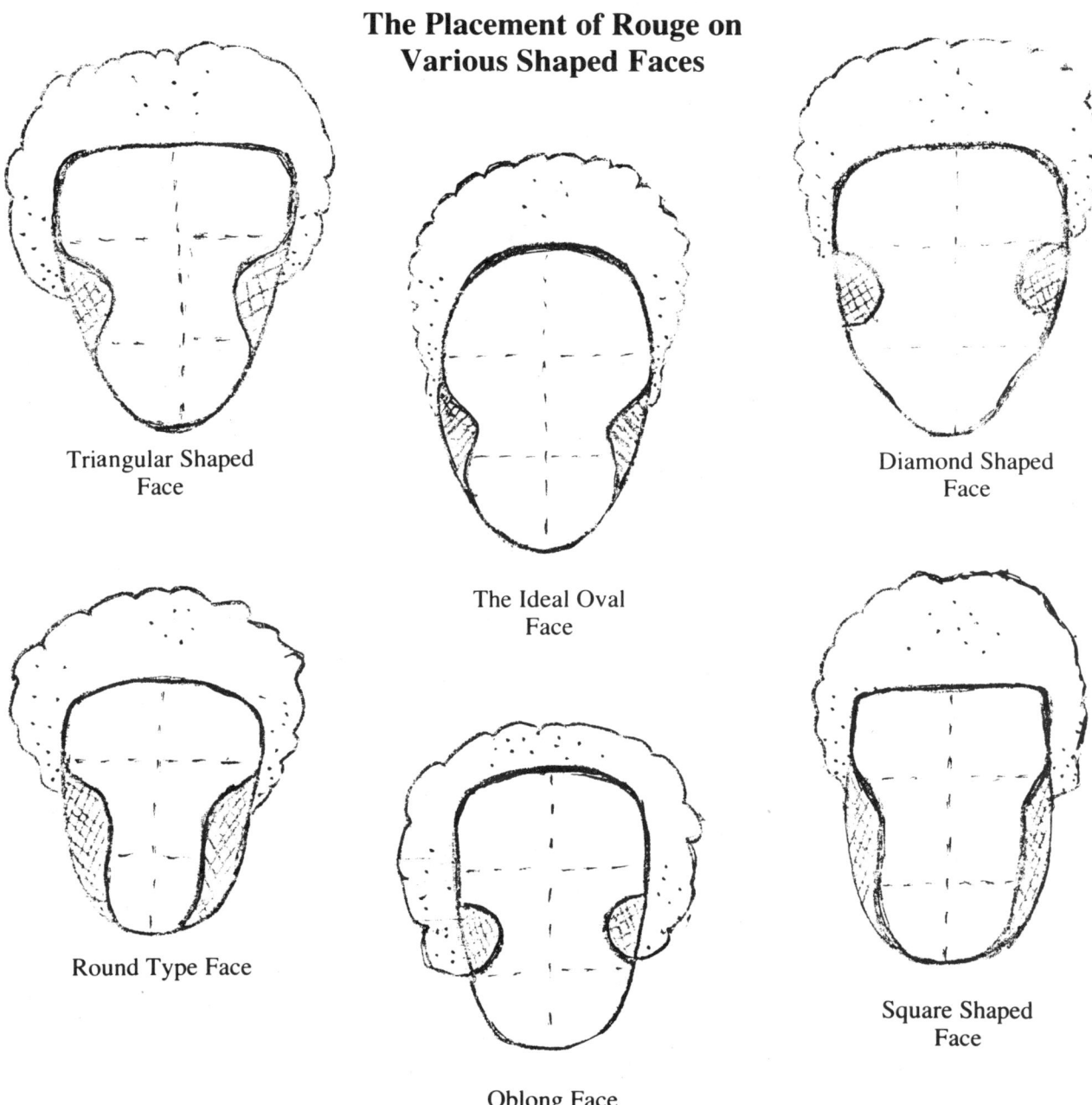

The Placement of Rouge on Various Shaped Faces

Triangular Shaped Face

The Ideal Oval Face

Diamond Shaped Face

Round Type Face

Oblong Face

Square Shaped Face

Youth to "Old Age"

It is a challenge to the makeup artist who has to transform a young person into an older one for the stage. Even more complex is the task of creating the illusion of old age in the young black performer.

Some biological facts concerning the aging process for people of darker skins, the black race in particular, are worth considering. They tend to fade or sallow with added years to colors of grays, olives, greens, or yellows. For the light complexed black, the skin will take on a deeper, darker, intense tone of his own skin color.

The negroid skin is inclined to age slowly because of the dark colored pigmentation protecting it from the harmful rays of the sun. It does not wrinkle rapidly, because of its ability to produce and maintain high contents of oil which preserves the skin's elasticity. Facial lines are slow in developing and do not appear prominently until the advent of very old age, perhaps eighty or over.

One should consider that it is simpler to transform a middle aged black person into an old one than to begin with a young actor. Conversely, it is easier to change a young person into an old one than to produce a younger character from an older one.

Effects of "lighting" on the Dark Complexioned actor

Another problem for the dark skinned actor is the effect light has upon him and his makeup. The primary colors of pigment are red, blue, yellow; whereas, in light the primary colors are red, green, and a deep blue. All three colors of light produce a white light or a shade like raw sunlight. Stage lights influence the color of makeup, and one should apply makeup under the color of light to be used on stage. At least check the makeup under the lights for the show in which the actor will perform.

Each color accents itself in makeup as well as in costumes and scenery. Red brightens red; blue brings out blue; and green heightens the green shades. They also effect other colors. Red will turn green to gray. Green will make red a blackish color. Blue will change red to purple. Blue or green will produce a bluish-green. The black actor's skin tone will be effected by special lights. Pinks will give him a warm brown skin tone. Blues and green will make him darker or grayer. Straw and yellow will seem to age his skin. Bastard amber (pink and straw) is best for his outdoor appearance; and pinks and lavenders make him look healthy on an indoor set. The dark skinned person will usually look better under shades of warm colors because any pigment will look grayish, or even black, if it does not contain any of the colors composing the ray of light which is used on it. A word of caution is that pure white light with no color in it has a tendency to wash out hues of makeup.

In general, amber lights are best suited for the black actor. Since there are such varieties of shades among black actors, no hard and fast rule of highlighting can be set down.

Special atmospheric scenes will demand the same type of lighting for the black actor as is true with actors of all races. Blue and green colored lights seem to de-emphasize or even eliminate the black character from the scene.

Stage lights change from one scene to another during performances, so one must be careful that they do not cause his makeup to vary in appearance. The careful artist will check his work under all the lights to be used on it.

Corrective Makeup

Certain corrective makeup can be accomplished. The teeth can cause a problem. For discolored or gold teeth, tooth enamel may be painted right on the tooth. For the actor who has scars or damaged skin nose putty or derma wax, tinted to the proper tone, can sometimes fill in the space. The eyes, mouth, eyebrows, and nose can be reshaped by makeup to give them a more pleasing appearance. The eyes can be enlarged by outlining them in white. They can be brightened by a reddish-dot placed at the inner corner next to the nose bridge. They can be made to seem wider by a small white dash at the outer corners. The nose can be shortened or lengthened by a lowlight or a highlight color placed beneath the tip of it by the nostrils. The nose can be made thinner by a highlight color extended down the ridge from the eyebrows to the tip. It can look broader with highlights running along each side of the nose. Lips can be narrowed or enlarged by the use of moist rouge. They can be outlined with a thin line of a darker color than the lip rouge. Many things can be done by makeup to improve appearances for characters in a play. It will take just a little experimenting to come up with the desired effect.

Areas of the nose which can be highlighted or lowlighted.

Thin lips can be painted within the bounds shown by the dash lines.

Thick lips can be thinned by using lip rouge within the dash lines.

For Your Notes

For Your Notes

CHAPTER II

PRINCIPLES GOVERNING THE USE OF MAKEUP

Dr. Allen Williams writes on the basic properties of stage makeup in his book, *A Theatre Handbook*. He asserts that with modern day dimmer systems and high wattage lamps the intensity of the lighting is so great that even with the black actor the natural facial attributes are weakened or washed out. Therefore, it is necessary that the appropriate makeup be applied to the actor for two reasons: first, to protect the skin from the strong rays, and second, to emphasize the natural features of the face or other areas of the body.

Through the application of makeup, the artist can give life to straight as well as to special characterizations and nationalities. In regular makeup, usually referred to as straight, little more is done than to strengthen the skin color and accent the facial structure. Much more than this can be achieved in character makeup by giving an actor a more youthful appearance or by creating the image of old age. Anything that alters the actor's looks to make him fit the role he is playing can be called character makeup. It can cover anything from beauty marks to grotesque scars.

Through the ultimate magic of makeup, the entire configuration of the facial structure and other visible parts of the body can be made to look different. Williams comprehensively states, "The makeup selected and the method of application are governed by the coloring and intensity of the stage lighting and the changes made necessary in order to represent the dominant facial characteristics of the part played."

A simple statement can be made from what has been said. Every stage actor must be made up to some degree for the protection of the skin and for the development of characterization. However, there is a principle which cannot be overlooked. The amount and kind of makeup are to an extent determined by the color and texture of one's skin and the intensity of the lights under which he performs.

Care of the Skin before and after Makeup Application

According to Mr. John A. Sampognaro, R.Ph., "Proper skin preparation is vital to an individual before and after makeup application." One must consider that stage makeup is much "heavier" than regular or street makeup.

Below is a list of simple steps governing preparation of the skin, with special emphasis and attention given to the troubled skin.

1. Cleanse the skin thoroughly using a mild soap such as Ivory (it is preferrable not to use a perfumed soap) with a soft turkish face cloth, massaging the face gently in a circular upward motion. The facial muscles are the least elastic of all the muscles of the body; therefore, improper downward cleans-

ing motions can cause premature sagging and wrinkles. Depending on skin temperature tolerance, the water should range from very warm to almost hot, in order to open the pores to permit deep cleansing of the skin's surface.

2. When this procedure is complete, rinse thoroughly with very cool to cold water to aid in closing the pores. Pat dry with a soft turkish towel.

3. At this point, apply a mild astringent lotion because it absorbs the oil on the skin surface, counteracts excessive perspiration, continues to clean, dry and protect the skin from other harmful agents. Apply the lotion to a sterile cotton ball and pat on to the face and allow it to dry before proceeding further. Proceed with caution when patting around the eyes, since astringents contain agents which can severely irritate or damage the eyes. Some suggested astringents are: O.J.'s Beauty Lotion, Witch Hazel, Coty, and agents by Revlon.

4. Finally, apply a cover agent to the skin in order to protect further the skin from harm that might be caused by heavy stage makeup. A recommendation is to use *Fostril* or *Fostex CM*, products which can be valuable in several ways: to aid in healing acne prone skin, to form a protective shield coat over the highly sensitive skin, and to use merely as a makeup "cover". These products are available at most drug stores.

To apply, follow the simple directions given on the tube. Use "The Dap Method" on the prominent areas of the face, one area at a time. It is important that one work fast, using quick upward strokes to smooth the agent out over the entire skin surface. Its quick-drying properties demands swift well executed motions of the fingertips.

At the completion of this procedure, the skin takes on a dry, translucent appearance. The face is now ready for the application of makeup.

Makeup Removal

The makeup should be removed immediately following a performance or as soon as possible. Remember, the skin likes to be kept clean and free from foreign agents which place undue stress or burdens on it. Therefore, it must soon be returned to its normal state.

Removing the makeup is a simple process when proper techniques are employed and the appropriate products are used.

Below are suggested steps to follow in removing makeup and the proper care of the skin after the makeup has been removed.

1. Select an appropriate cold cream for one's skin type. For the hypersensitive, troubled skin, hypoallergenic cleansing creams are available, such as: allercreme, marcelle, and abalene cream
2. Apply cold cream to the area to be cleansed. Remove it with a few soft facial tissues. If this is insufficient to cleanse the skin, repeat the process.
3. To complete the care of the skin, use warm water and a soft turkish towel. Wash with a good facial soap or a medicated soap such as Cuticura. Rinse thoroughly with cool water and pat dry with a soft terry cloth towel. For further care of the hypersensitive skin one may apply the protective covering called Fostril.

The Art of Applying Foundation Color

Both men and women should pull the hair back from the face or cover it with a cloth down to the hair line. In addition to this men should be clean shaven.

Because of the oily, porous nature of the darker skin it should be cleaned thoroughly by washing and dried by patting with a turkish towel. To create a smooth skin surface and to close the pores, apply with a cotton ball, an astringent such as Witch Hazel or O.J.'s Beauty Lotion. This also aids in the removal of oil from the skin and counteracts perspiration.

When the face is completely dry, use your fingers to rub a small amount of cold cream over the skin. Remember to cover the forehead, eye sockets, eye lids, nose, ears, and throat. Pat the face with a soft tissue to absorb excessive amounts of cold cream.

One word of caution concerning cold cream. It should not be used at all if the base coat is to be a greasepaint. There is already enough grease in the paint for easy application and anything more would be in excess of what is needed.

At this point it is time to choose the desired foundation color for a specific makeup requirement. Base paint comes in tubes, cakes, sticks, and bottles. Liquid makeup, which comes in bottles, can be used for the body as well as the face.

The dark skinned person seldom needs a base paint because his skin is already richly colored. If, however, his skin is light he may wish to darken it. If he is assigned the role of a nationality other than his own, he will want to change the skin tone to suit the character.

THE APPLICATION OF FOUNDATION COLOR

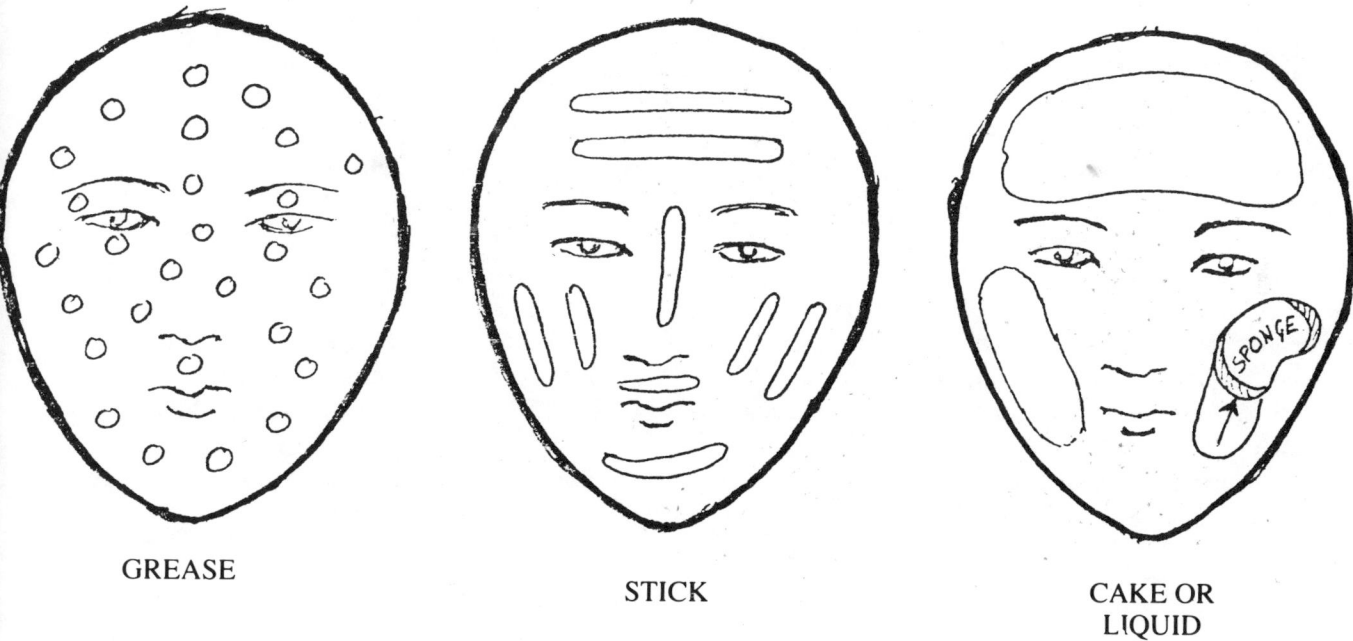

GREASE   STICK   CAKE OR LIQUID

Foundation Paint

When the foundation to be used is grease paint, apply the color by dotting it over the entire face and then spreading it evenly by circular upward motions of the fingers. Do not forget to make up the ears, neck, and hands. After the grease base has been applied, it should be rubbed with tissue in order to remove any excess makeup. It is the grease in the extra makeup which causes an actor to "shine." Care must be taken that too much highlight line is not applied, for it also gives a greasy appearance, even under the best powder.

Stick makeup is put on in even strokes across the neck, face and hands. Smooth out the paint with your fingers until the desired area to be covered is one continuous color. A little cold cream will help this.

Liquid and cake makeup are laid on with a damp sponge and spread smoothly across the area being made up. These, as well as the other base colors, should be used sparingly; one is painting the skin and not building up a mask. Be sure to cover the forehead, eye sockets, and ears and smooth the paint over the edge of the chin and jawbone, allowing the color to blend out onto the throat and neck.

Some appendages which may need to be added to the skin must be put on before a base coat of makeup has been applied. Such additions as nose putty and derma wax will not adhere to the skin if makeup is present. The face should also be left clean for the placement of spirit gum or latex to secure crepe hair for beards, sideburns and eyebrows.

Face Powder

Face powder need not be as dark as the actor's complexion. Stein's powders #2 and #43 are good for makeup which stress the pink tones. Stein's powders #7 and #12 may be used for the amber tones. The powder must be used generously and allowed to set before the excess is removed.

Nose Putty and Derma Wax

Nose putty and derma wax can be used for both flat and extended appendages, attached to the skin. They may be used separately or together. Nose putty is used by itself for lifting or enlarging sections of the face, such as noses, ears, and chins, or for creating warts and lascerations of the skin. Derma wax can also be used for these purposes but is not strong enough to stand on its own under the demands of stage acting. When mixed with nose putty (even half and half) the end product is easier to mold and holds up much better. Both nose putty and derma wax comes in colors of pink or neutral and must be mixed with a dye in order to blend with brownish skin tones. No shades of putty are made for the black actor.

Derma wax is a tool of the mortician's trade sometimes borrowed for use by the makeup artist. In order to match the color of the wax to darken skin tones, Eddie Douzart, a mortician, says "Blending of color is much less a problem than it used to be, because now derma wax is available in chocolate brown, orange, neutral, and white. To achieve a desired color knead any two or three combinations together." Derma wax and tinting materials may be purchased from any funeral supply house.

After the nose putty or derma wax has been applied to the skin and molded to a specific shape, paint it with a base coat of makeup being used.

During a stage performance, perspiration and oily secretions may decrease the ability of the putty wax to adhere to the skin. It is necessary to check between scenes for needed repairs.

Hair and Beards

Hair is a growth out of the epidermus of mammals forming a coat over all or on certain body areas of the animals. The human animal has three kinds of hair: straight, curly and kinky.

Straight hair is long and usually coarse and round. It is nearly always black. American Indians, Chinese, Japanese and Mongols have hair of this nature.

Curly hair is oval in cross section and is the hair of the European. the colors vary from black to brown and there is red and blond.

The basic negro race possesses hair that is kinky, crinkly, coarse and short; it is generally termed "wooly." A divided section of this kind of hair would show it to be flattened or elliptical. It is naturally blackish and is seen on most black people except the native Australians and those of India whose hair is curly or straight. Today, the hair of the black American often deviates from the hair of the basic negro.

Gray hair is caused by a lack of color pigment appearing in the roots of the hair. A total absence of pigment produces white hair. White hair when not properly cleaned and cared for will appear yellowish.

Graying or whitening the hair can be accomplished in one of several ways: silver or white aerosol spray, white mascara, white shoe polish, or cornstarch. Powdering the hair, even with cornstarch, is the least effective means of graying it.

If need be, black hair can be changed to another color. It can be sprayed blond, if another color such as red is used first to form a base for an even covering.

Cross Sections of Hair

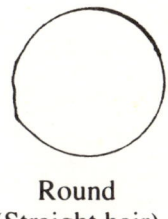 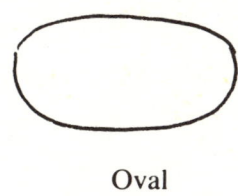 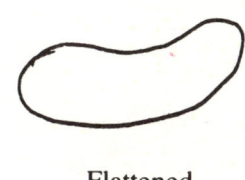

Round
(Straight hair)

Oval
(Curly hair)

Flattened
(Kinky hair)

Spirit gum, latex and crepe hair

Very few dark skinned people have light colored beards unless they are gray. There are light complexioned blacks who have blond hair, but they are rare. Most blacks will have black or dark brown hair.

Crepe hair is ideal for the negro's facial hair. All beards, even on whites, are curly and crepe hair comes in a plaited rope which keeps it kinky. It can be straightened out by dampening and stretching it over a period of time.

Spirit gum makes a good adhesive because it is clear and shows the skin under the hair.

Latex is used when a beard or hair piece is to be used over again. The latex holds the crepe hair in place and can be applied to the face again and again with little or no repair. Usually it will not bear close examination because the latex will be visible.

Spread the glue over the desired area upon which the hair is to be placed. Do this a little at a time because the adhesive dries rather rapidly. Be careful to cut the crepe hair and comb it out so it looks real. Do not use too much hair. A man's face has only so much space on it to grow a beard. Blacks usually do not have heavy facial hair anyway. This also goes for the almost beardless American Indian and the straggly and straight bearded Chinese. One interesting point of observation is that the black man's hair is just about the same all over his body. A caucasian may have straight hair on the head and a curly or straight beard.

In applying hair to the face it must appear to be coming out of the skin—not lying flat against it. Hair is added first under the chin, then to both sides of the jaws and up the side of the face for a full beard. The mustache usually has an opening in the hair at the center of the lip even though some mustaches grow straight across the whole lip.

Usually hair does not grow directly under the tip of the nose.

After the hair is placed on the face, pluck out the loose ends and trim the beard and mustache.

For Your Notes

CHAPTER III

THE YOUTHFUL LOOK

The look of youth is often called straight makeup in the theatre. It is not because one is young, so much as it is that one has a healthy appearance given to him by the makeup intended to enhance his normal looks under the stage lights. The actor is made up to look like himself.

Begin with a clean face so that there is no dirt, old makeup, or body oil to interfere with the application of the stage makeup. Most blacks will need little or no base makeup, because their skin color is less likely to be washed out by the bright lights.

Straight makeup for a young woman

A young woman without makeup

1. The Model's color is medium brown with regular facial features requiring little or no corrective makeup.

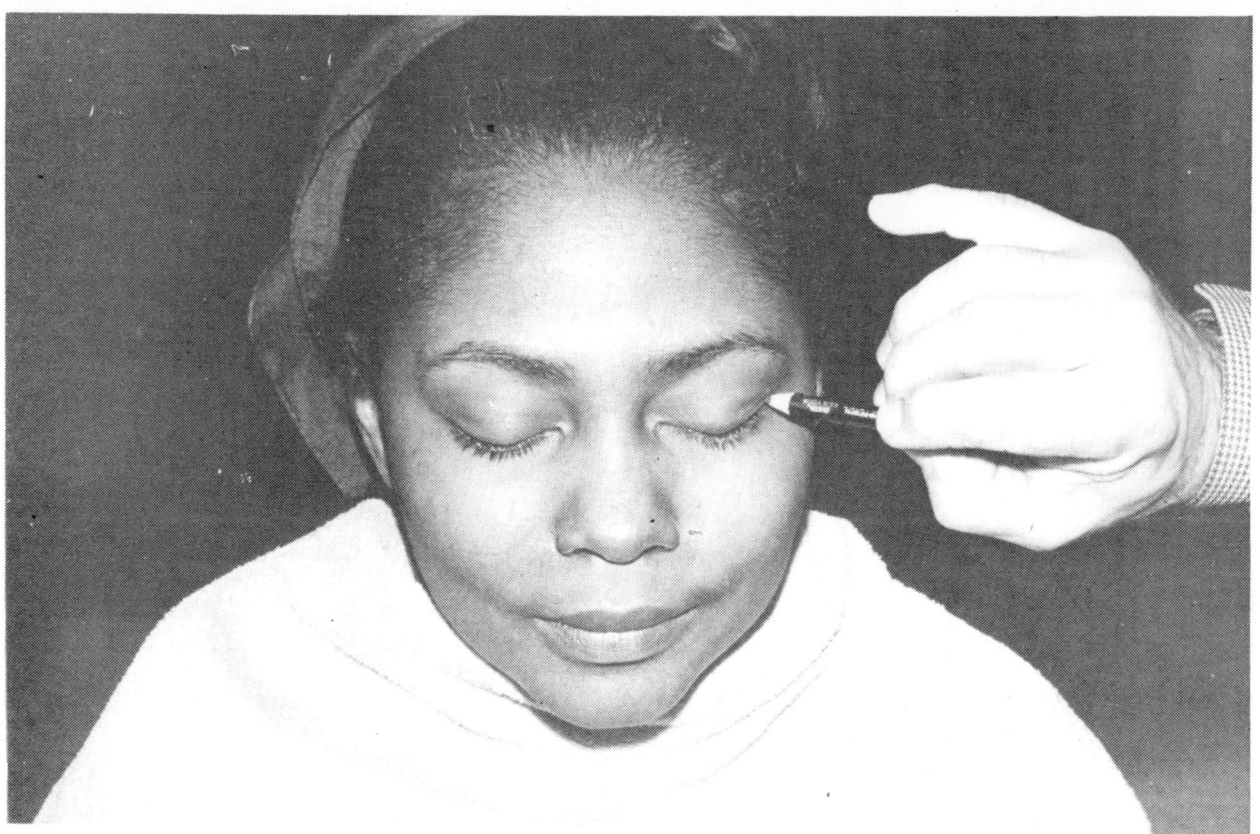

2. Lining the eyes and eyebrows with a black derma pencil. The line is carried all the way across the lid of the upper eye close to the lashes. The bottom lid line should be started from the center of the eye and drawn to the outer edge. It will give the eye a soft appearance. The eye can be made to seem harder by painting the line all the way across the lower lid. The natural lines of the eyebrow are followed.

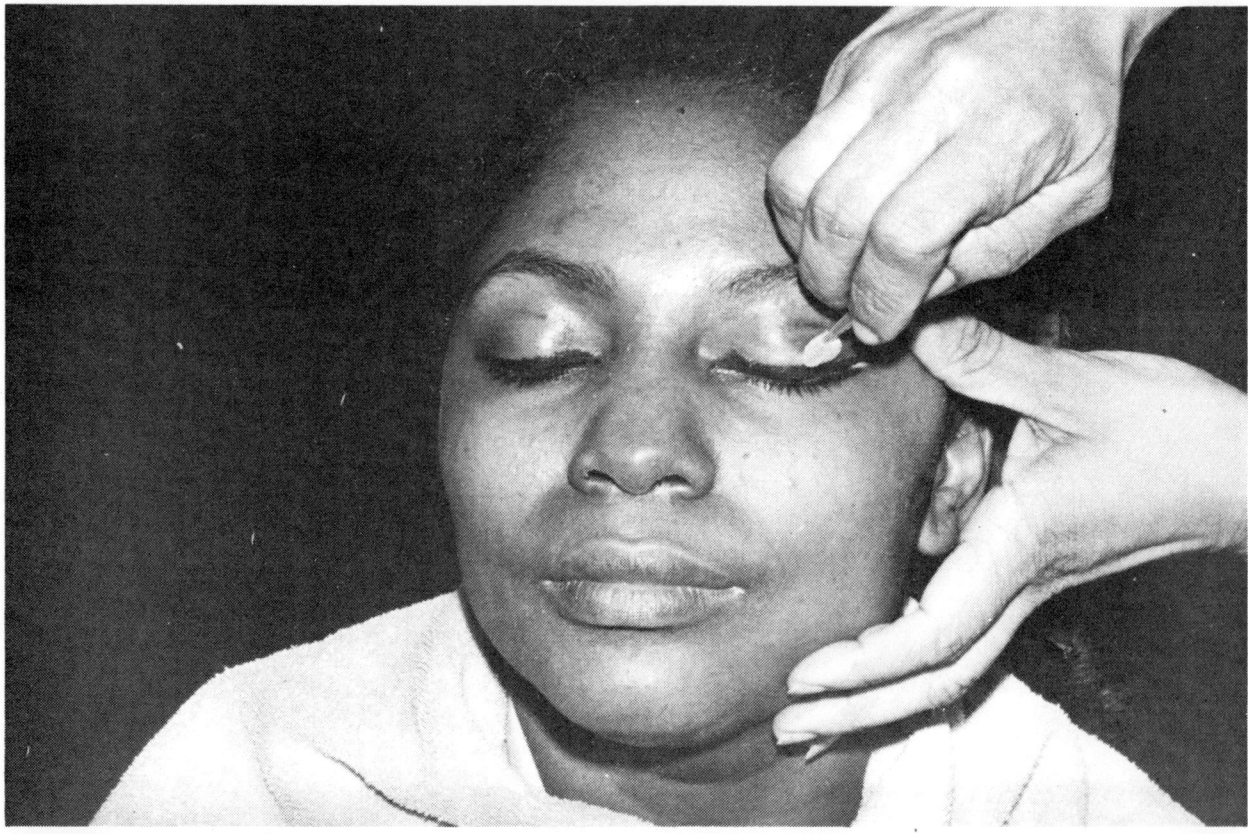

3. Applying plum colored shading to the eyelids. Place the paint along the lash lines and blend upward and outward toward the eyebrow and temple.

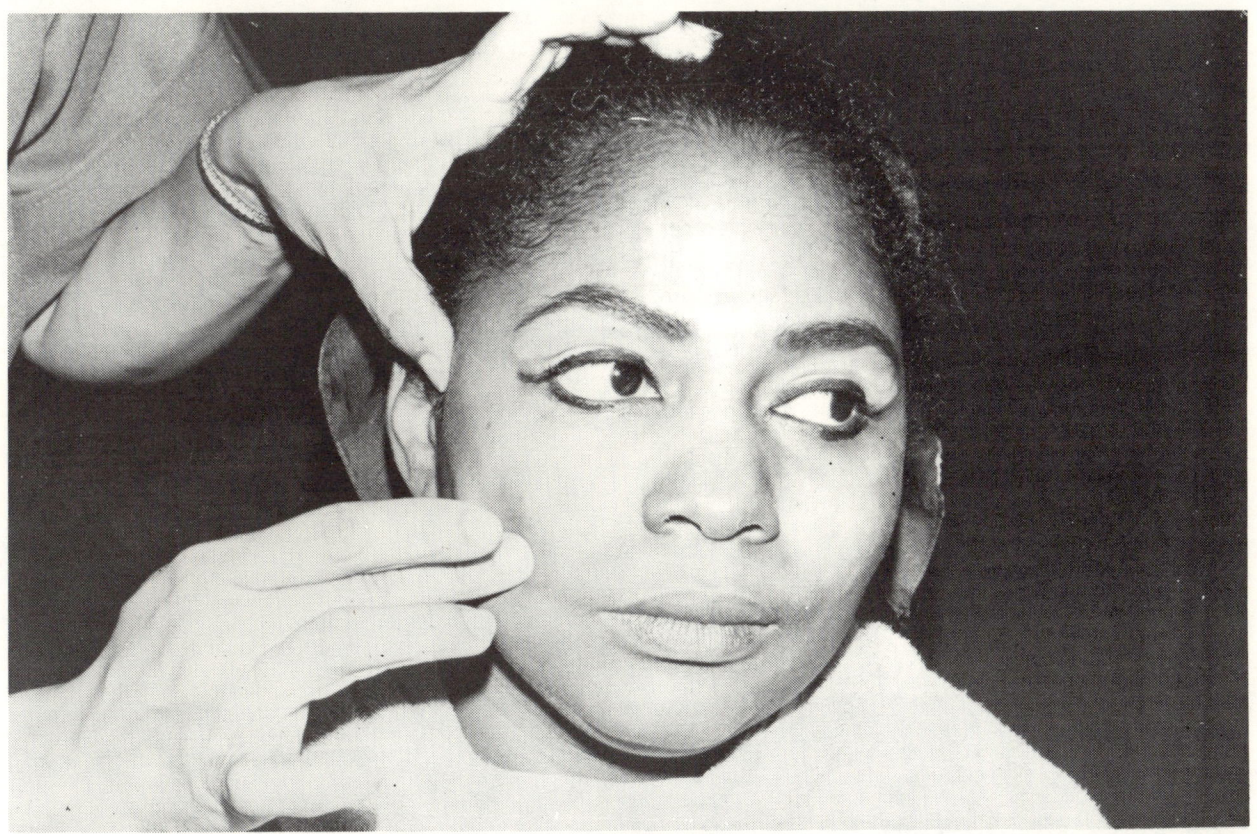

4. Rouge is applied to the cheeks and lips. A dark rouge helps to sink the cheekbones and gives a warm glow to the skin. Lip rouge brings out the natural shape and color of the lips.

5. The straight female makeup completed.

Straight makeup for a young man

Normally the basic negro male is characterized by dark-brown skin and kinky hair. He usually is erect in statute and virtually hairless except for the top of the head. The skull is ovoid in contour as seen from above. The forehead is broad. The cheeks are wide and the eyes are set apart. The nose is almost flat and the nostrils are expanded. The face is full and prominent. The jaws are powerful and have full lips which are reddish brown or purplish in color. Of course, these basic features vary when races mix and Asian and European characteristics blend with the black types.

Straight makeup must follow the natural shape of the actor's features in order to make the character look his best. An individual with regular facial formation need only accent his appearance. In most cases no base makeup is used because there is already color enought in the dark skin.

Do not overuse makeup on straight male characters or they will not look realistic.

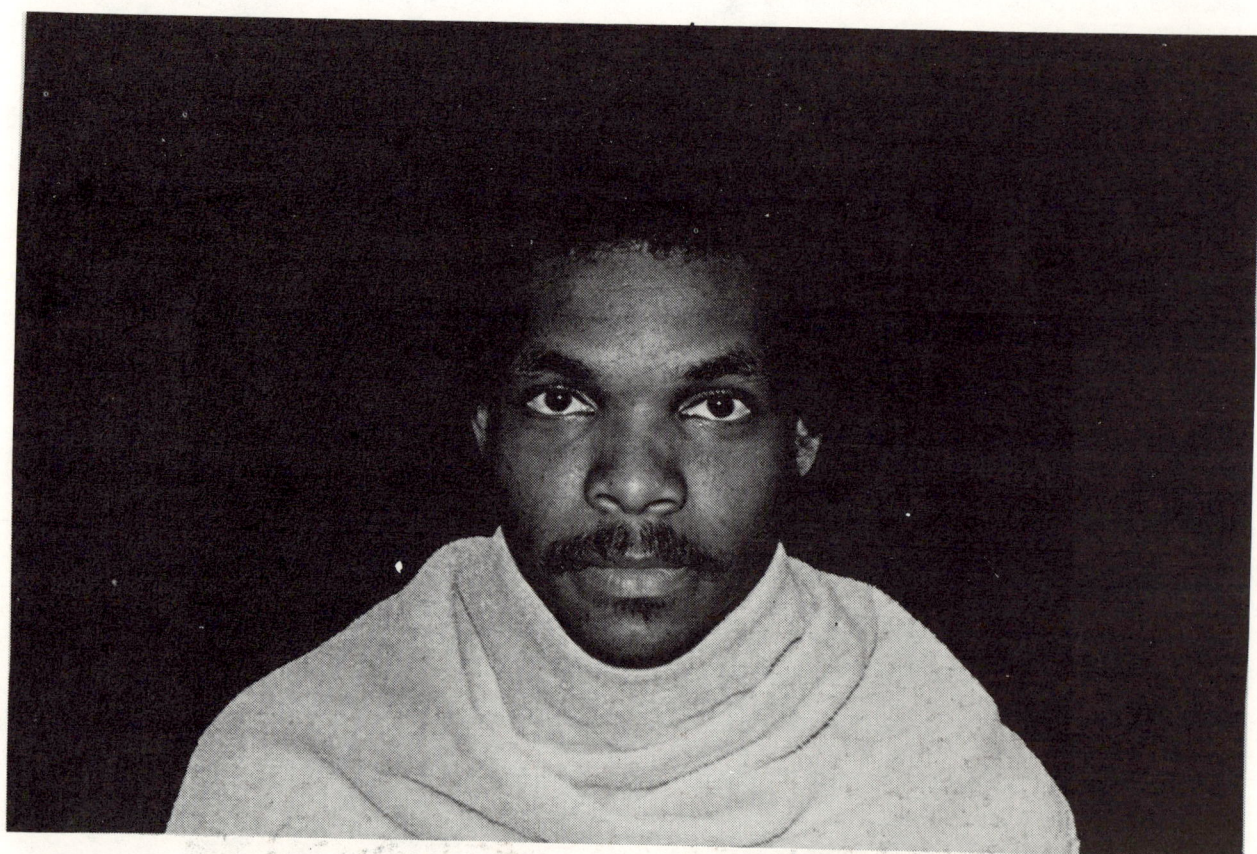

1. Young man with no makeup. The face has been cleansed and is ready for makeup. The model's coloring is a light brown.

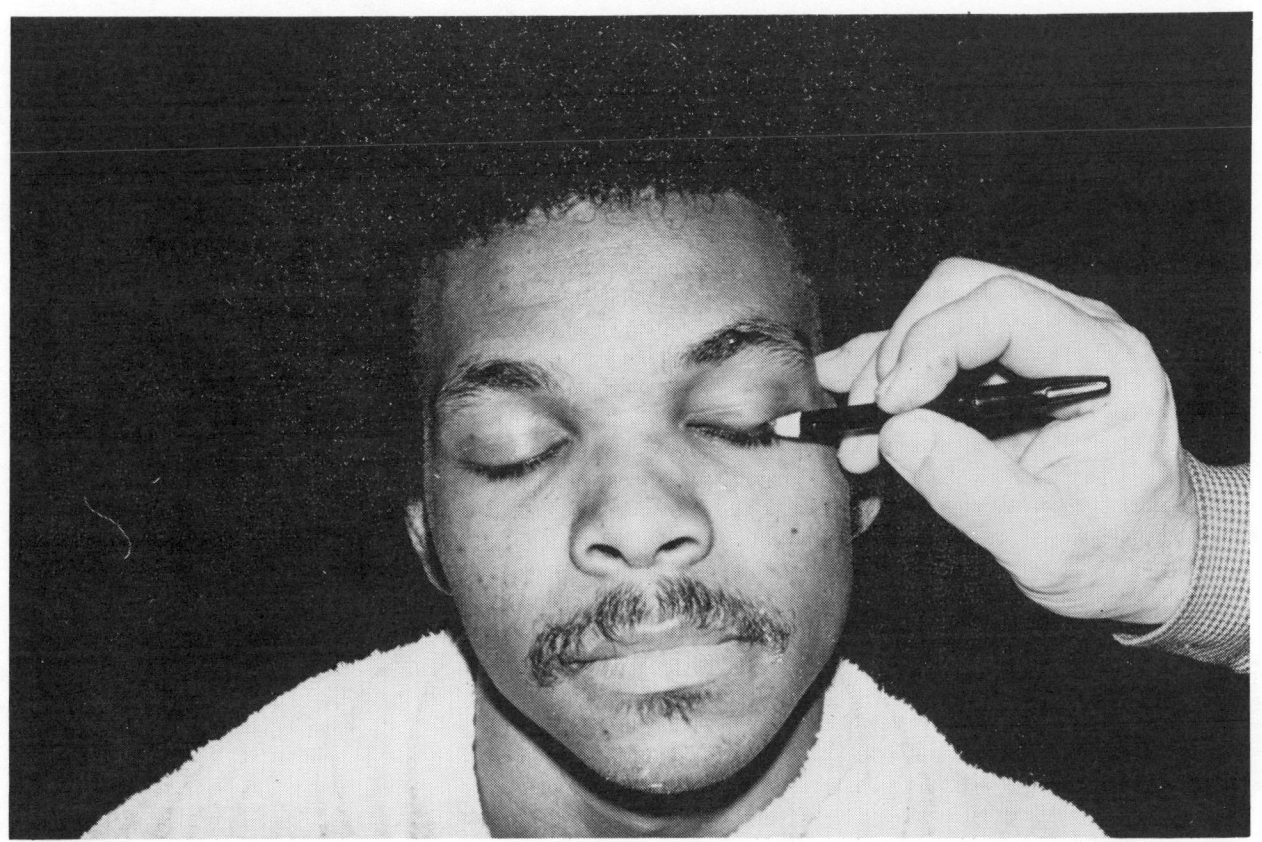

2. Lining the eyes and the eyebrows with a dark brown derma pencil by following the natural lines of the lashes and the eyebrows.

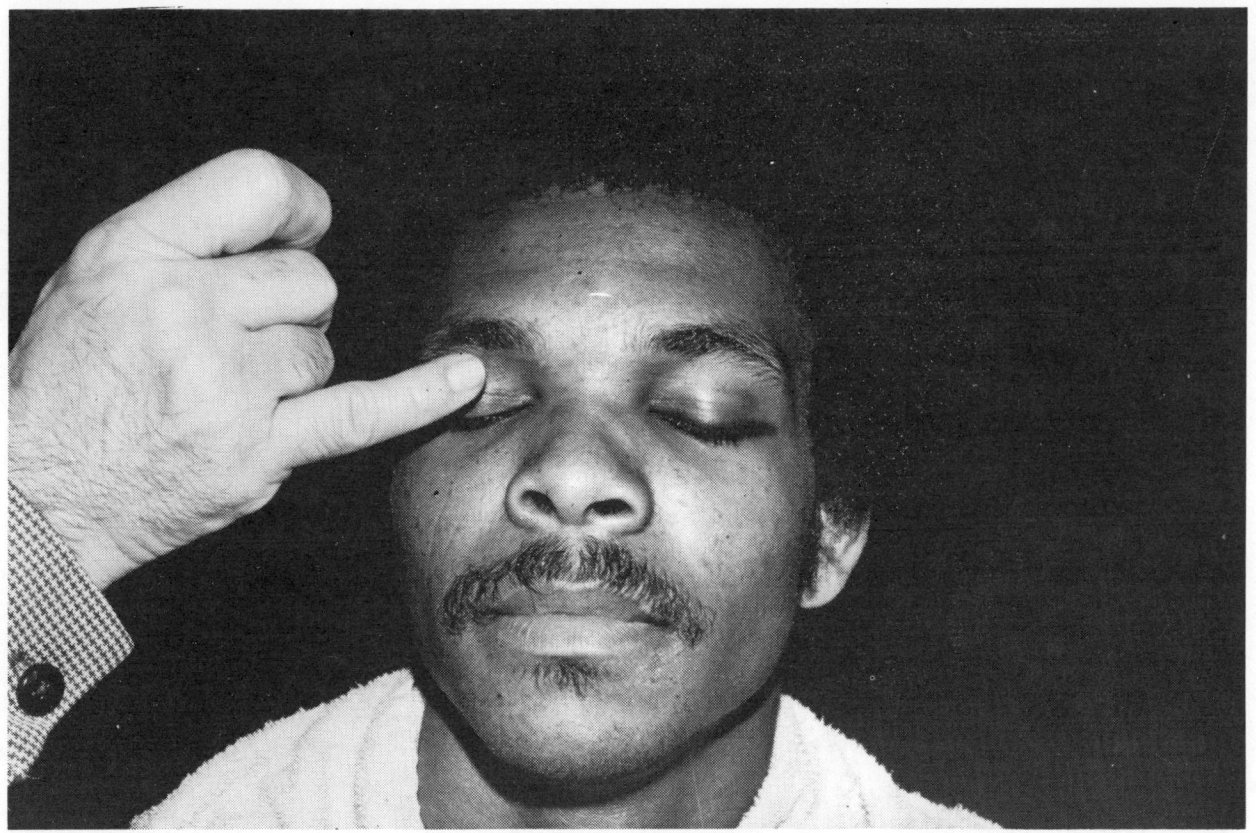

3. Shading the eyes with brown shadow. Start at the lashes and blend upwards to the brow and toward the temple.

4. Darkening and shaping the eyebrows with a dark brown eyebrow pencil. For regular straight makeup follow the natural eyebrow lines.

5. Adding a brownish red rouge to the cheeks.

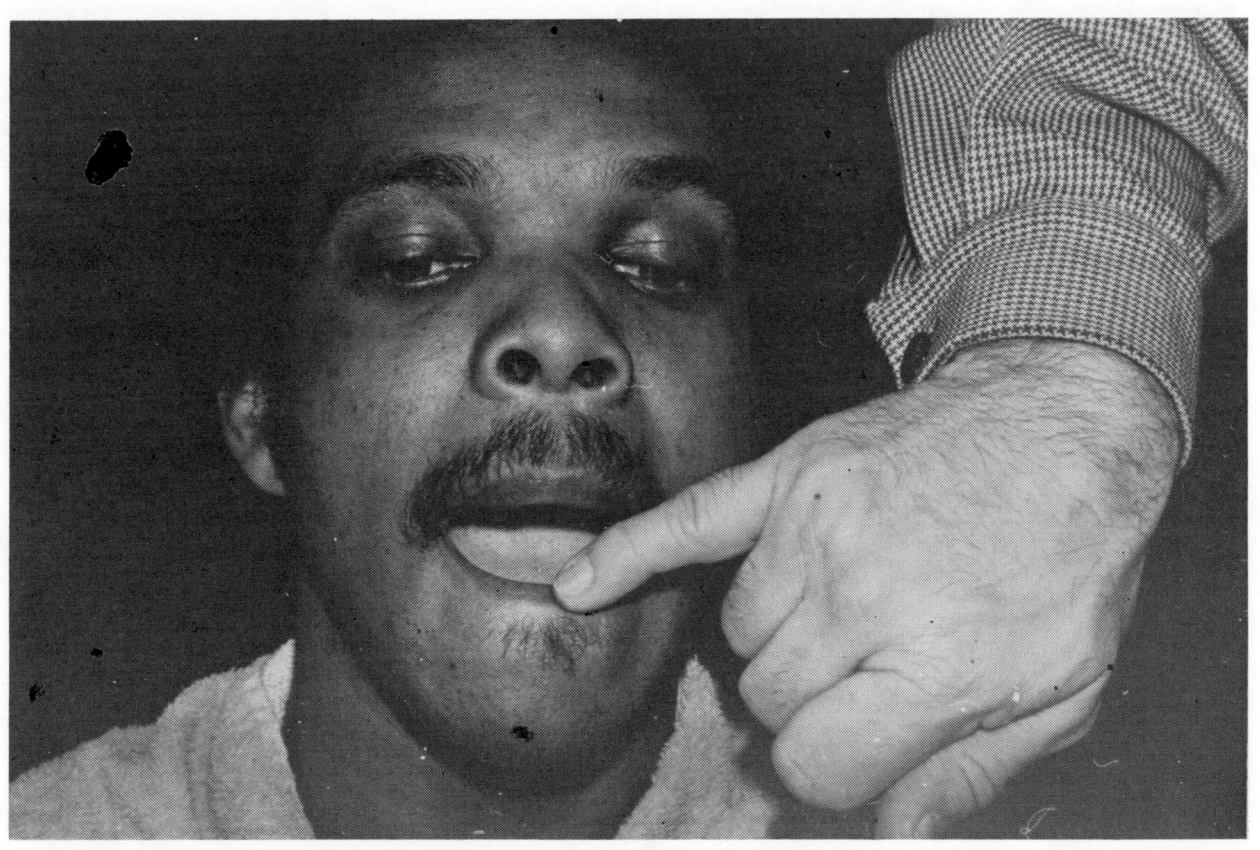
6. Moist brownish red rouge covers the natural shape of the lips.

7. Smudging the mustache with a dark brown derma pencil.

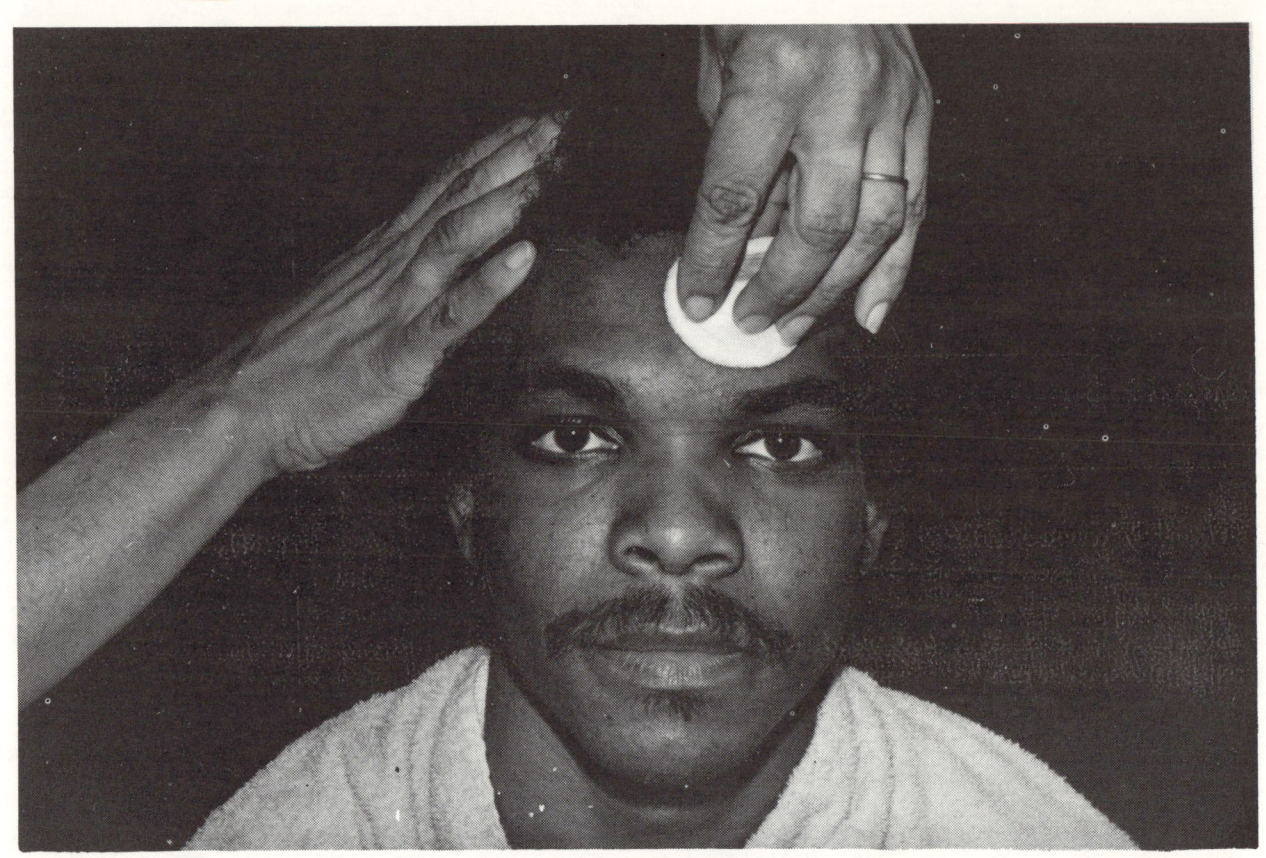

8. Setting the makeup with a natural colored powder.

9. The straight male makeup completed.

For Your Notes

For Your Notes

Chapter IV

MIDDLE AND OLD AGE MAKEUP

Half a century of living brings one to the old age of youth and the youth of old age.
— George Brian

The Psychological approach to making up older characters

Often times the young mind sees increasing age as a steady physical disintegration, a slow but consistent progression to a reclining position. Excluding injury or deformity, which has nothing to do with old age, the human body tends to become more erect with the passing of years. The older person seems to have more understanding and authority. The shoulders are firmly set, the arms and head more poised and the whole anatomy strains up from a straight spine.

For the sake of reality the actor who is to portray a person older than himself should look around and see the characteristics of aging people. Observation is the key word here. He should make comparisons of the sitting, standing and walking of the normal middle aged or old persons to that of his own age group. He will probably find that his conception of what should be happening and what is actually taking place are quite different. One of several things that will be noticed is stance. Old men generally place the center of their weight on their heels, while old ladies stand with their weight on the balls of their feet. Another is that older people move more slowly than younger ones. Still another observation is that the mature person speaks more surely with a voice of authority. Of course, not all middle aged and old persons are poised and settled at all times. Every age has its upsets, frustrations and conflicts. That is what drama is about.

What has all this to do with stage makeup? It needs to be impressed upon the student and the performer that it is possible for the human being to increase in stature rather than decrease as the years pass. This spirit must be reflected in the appearance of many older characters as the makeup artist plies his trade.

The playwright's characters in a play will indicate what type of person the actor is to portray. Some people become spiritually old before their time while others are still young at seventy and even later. Those who age in a dignified manner display a sparkling eye, vocal reserve, a youthful arrangement of silvery-gray hair, and assume an upright posture. For others the physical body sags in youth and the mind reaches old age early in life. The play script is the blueprint for such character makeup.

The use of the above approach to older character roles is valid for all races and nationalities. In this book however, special attention is given to middle and old age makeup for the dark skinned actor.

Old age makeup for a woman

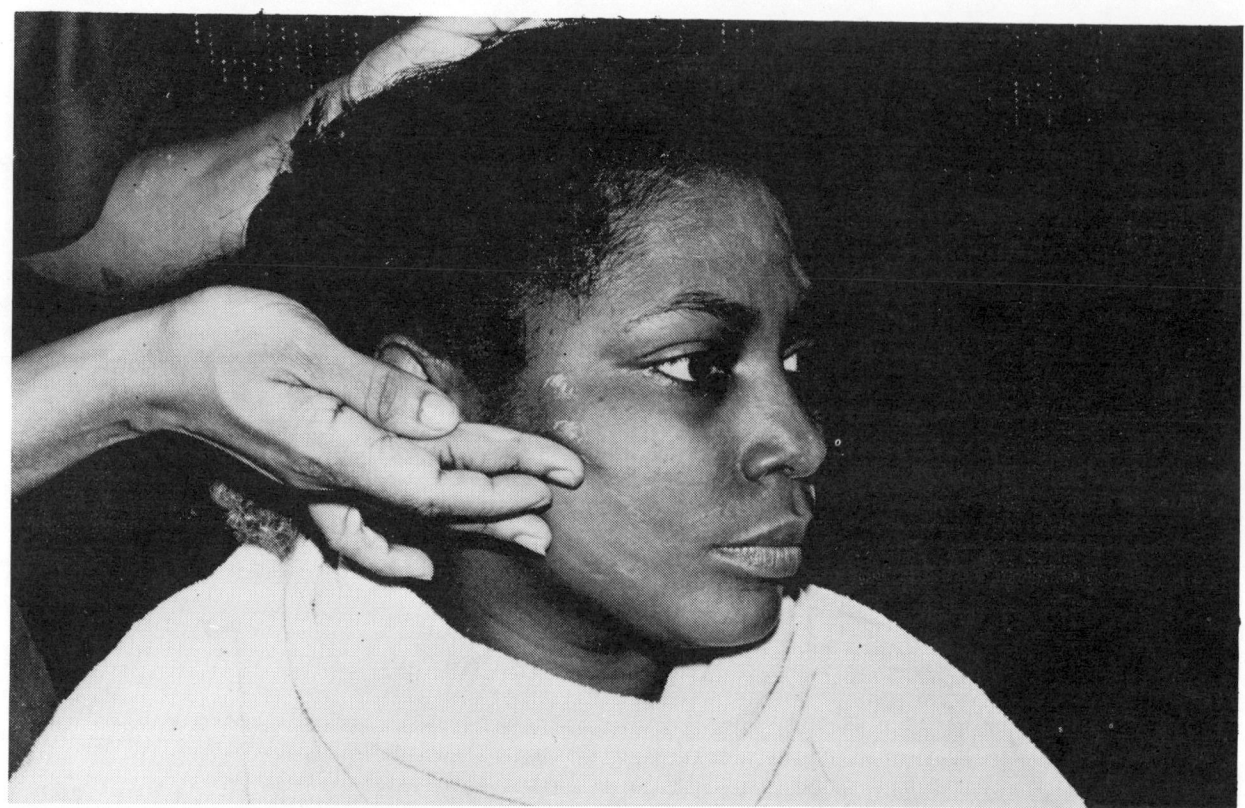

1. Blending a base of yellowish, olive brown color over the face and neck to give a sallow tone to the skin.

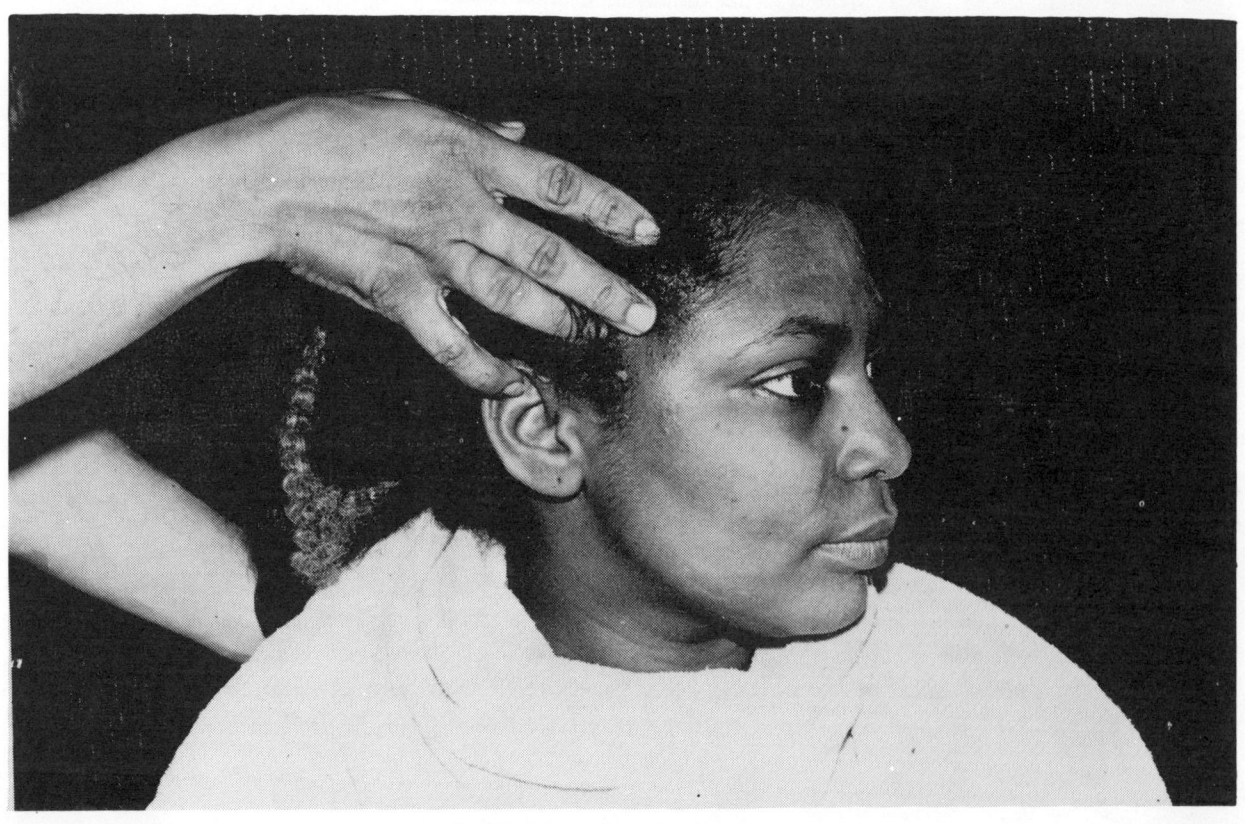

2. The completed base coat.

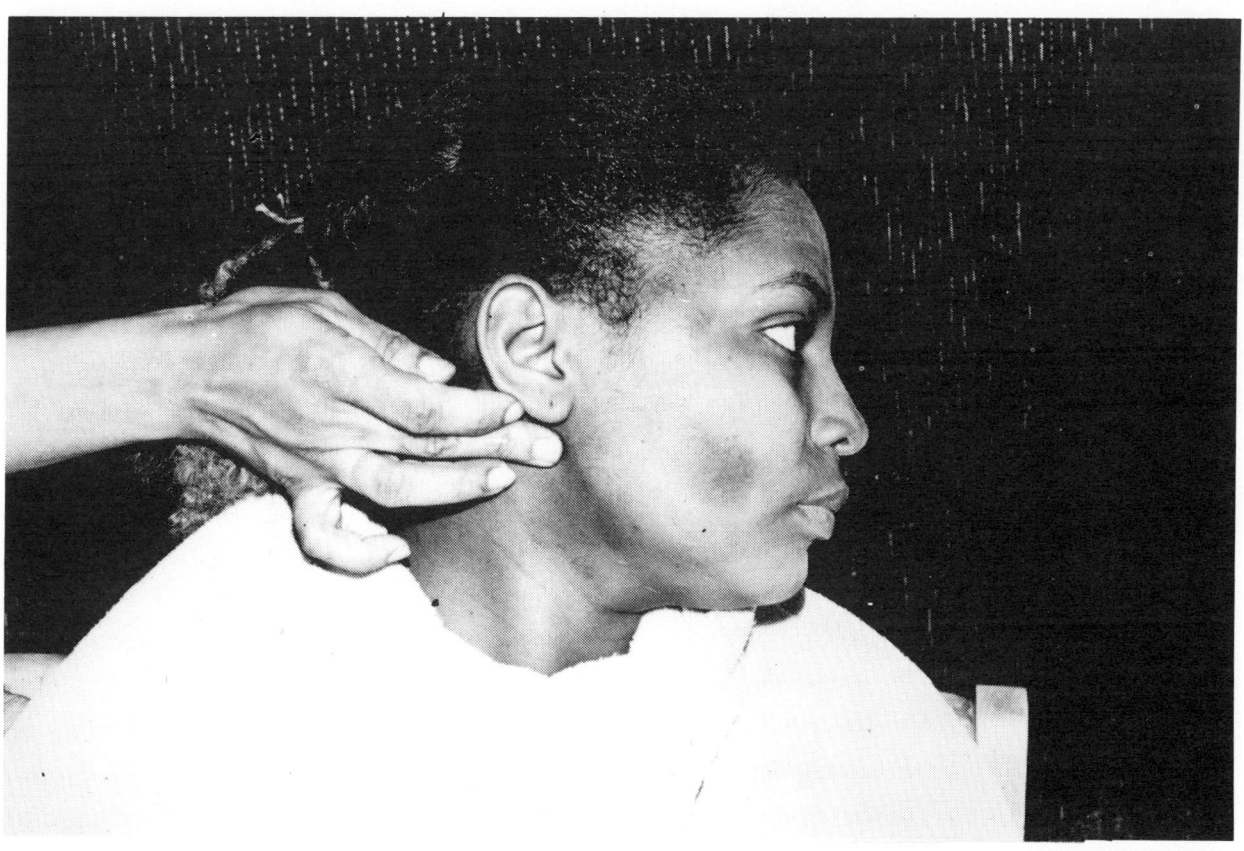

3. Dark brown lowlights are added to the sunken parts of the face and neck.

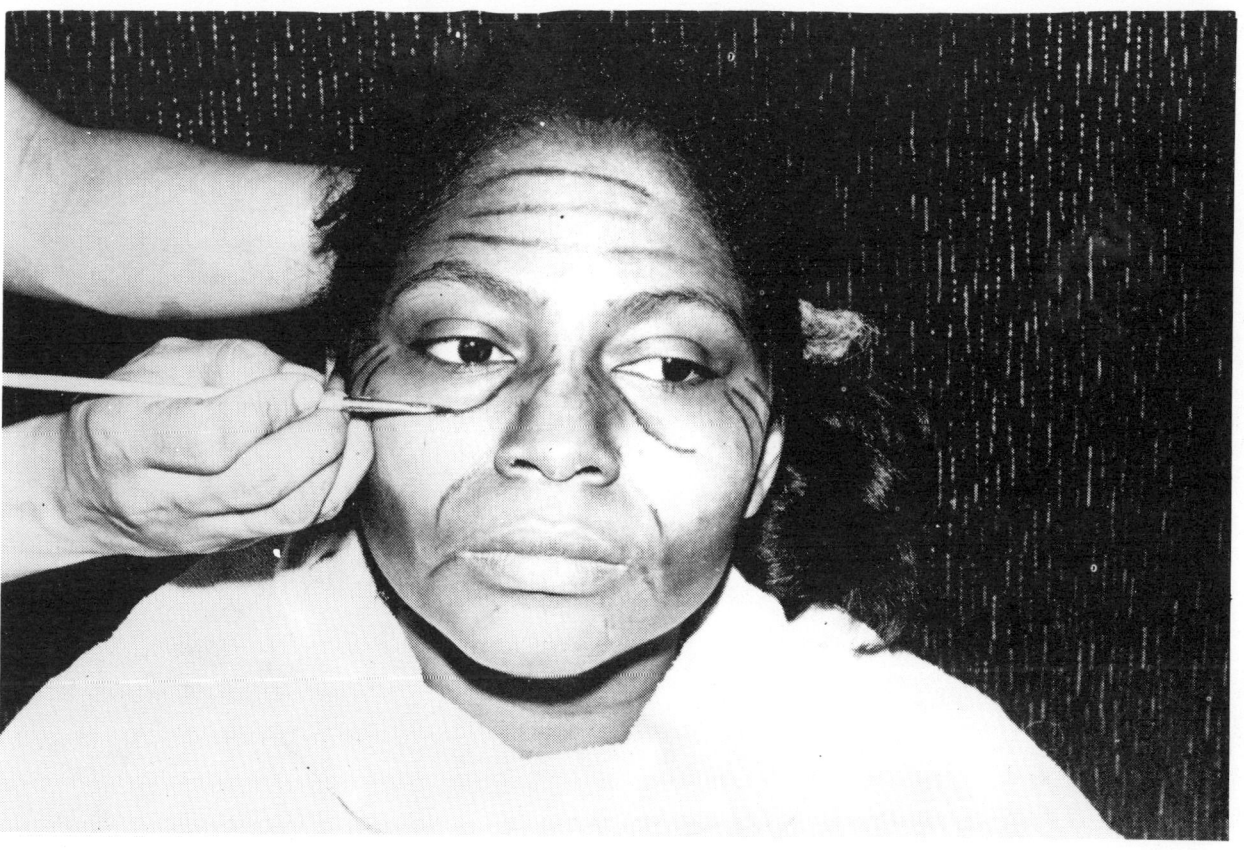

4. The painting of dark brown lines for wrinkles.

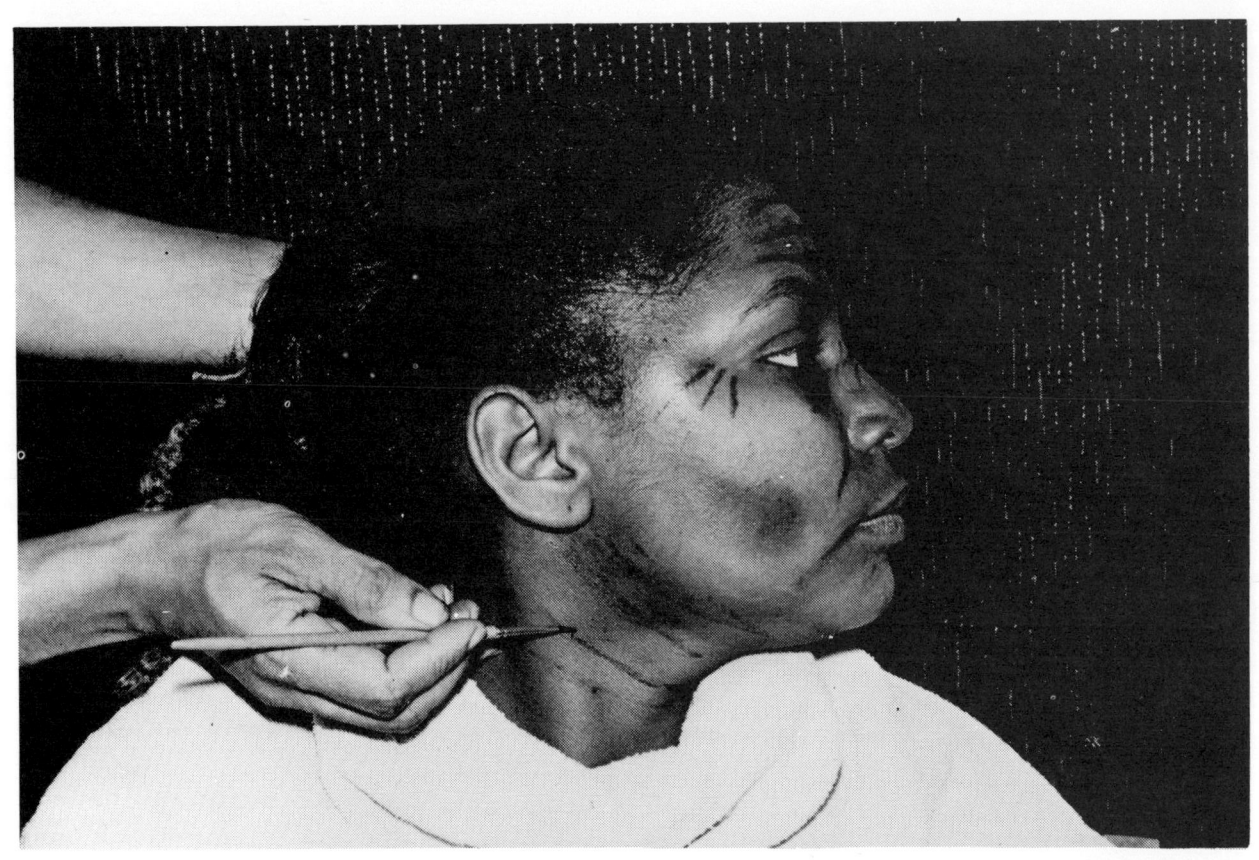
5. The application of lines on the neck.

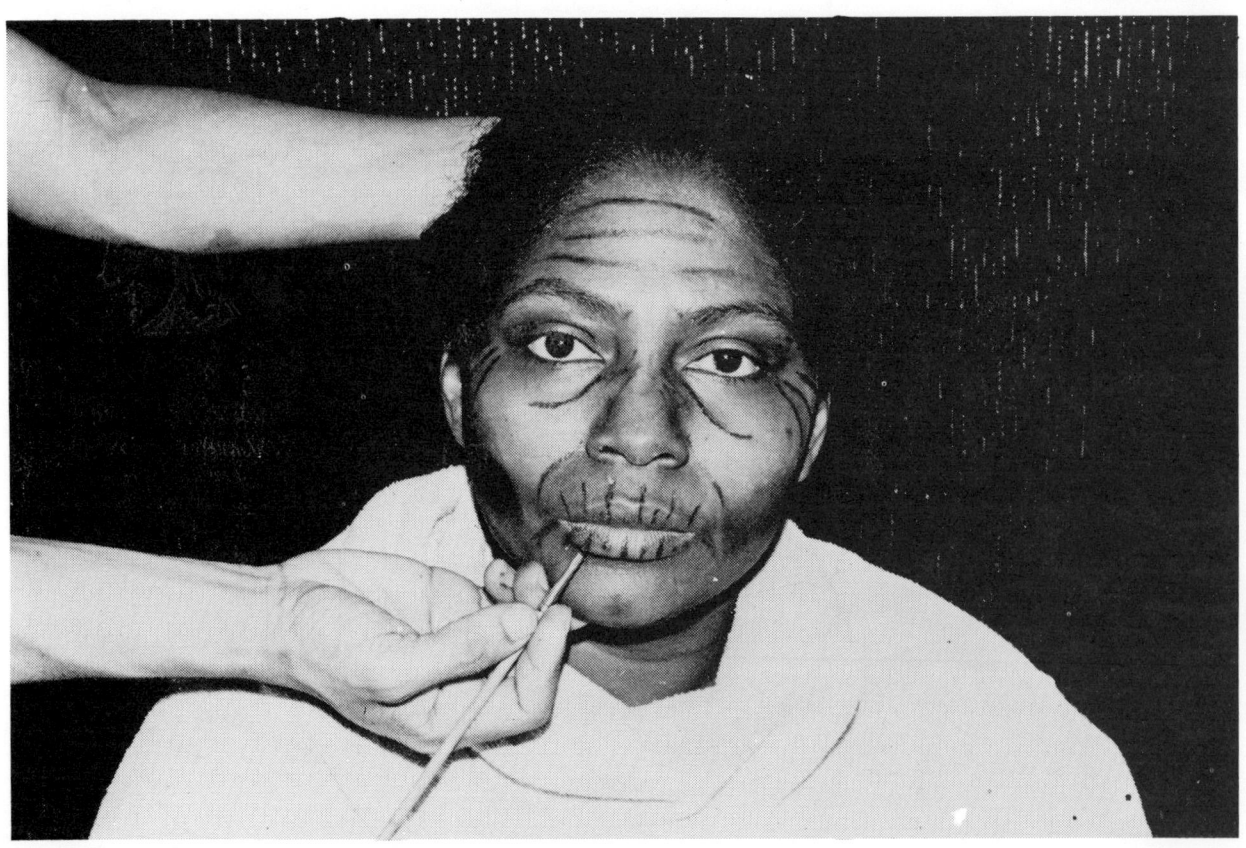
6. Lips are also lined for age.

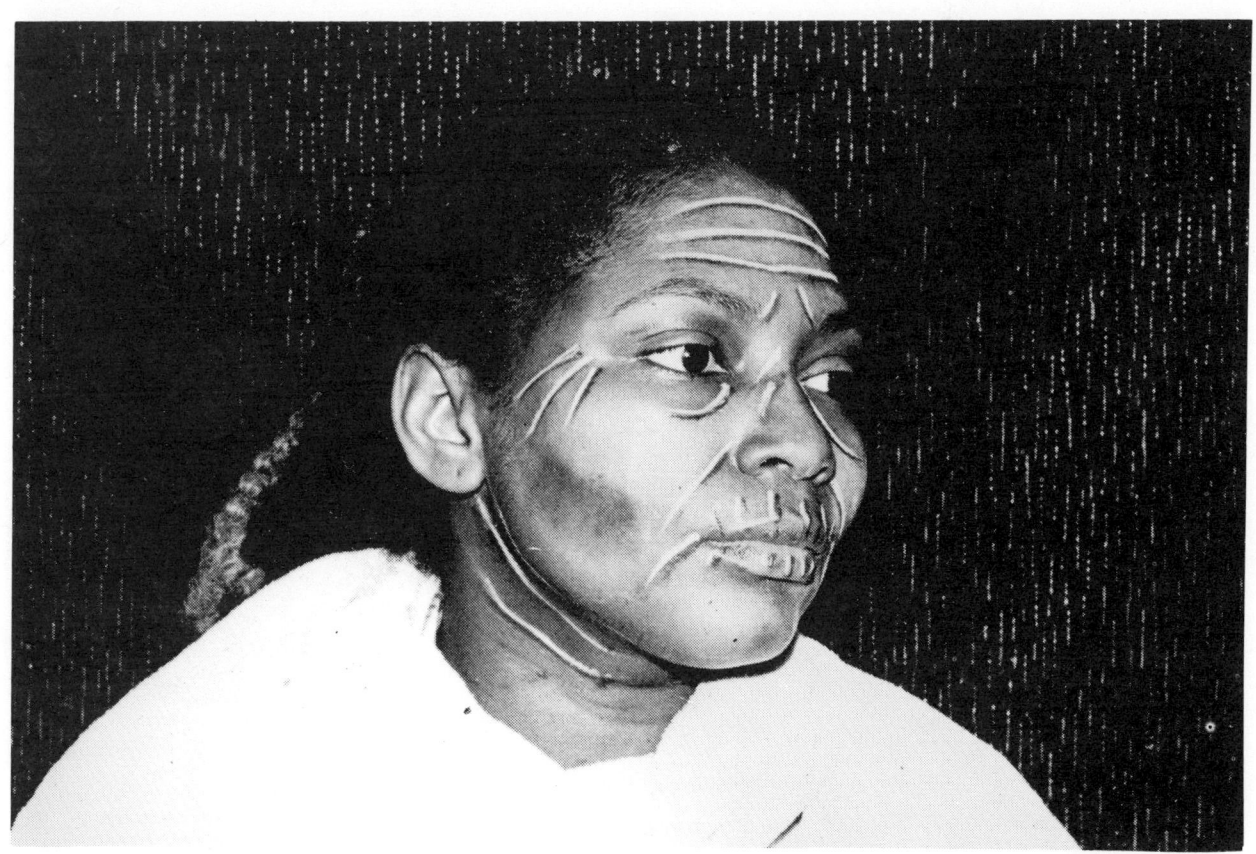
7. Yellow liner is added for highlights.

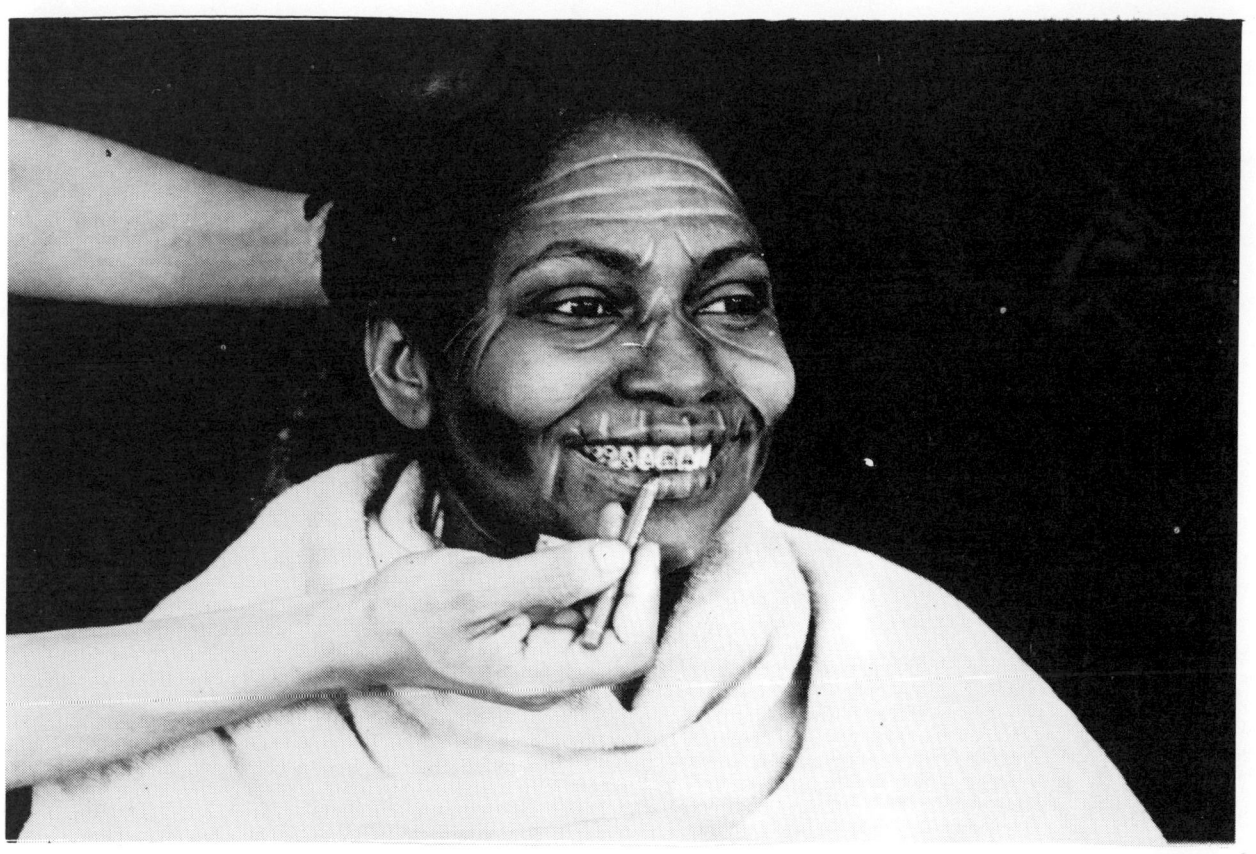
8. Teeth are aged and stained with a dark derma pencil. It is easily removed with tissue.

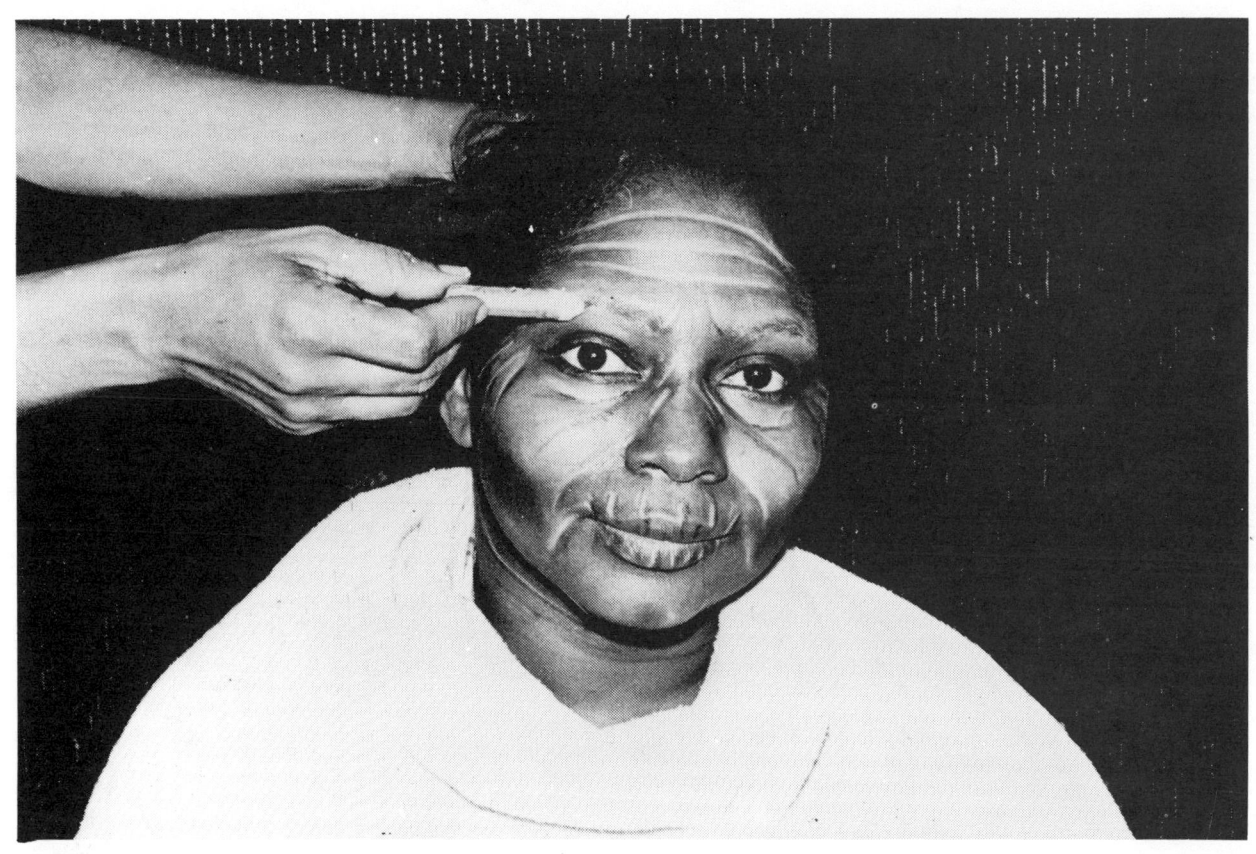

9. Eyebrows are whitened.

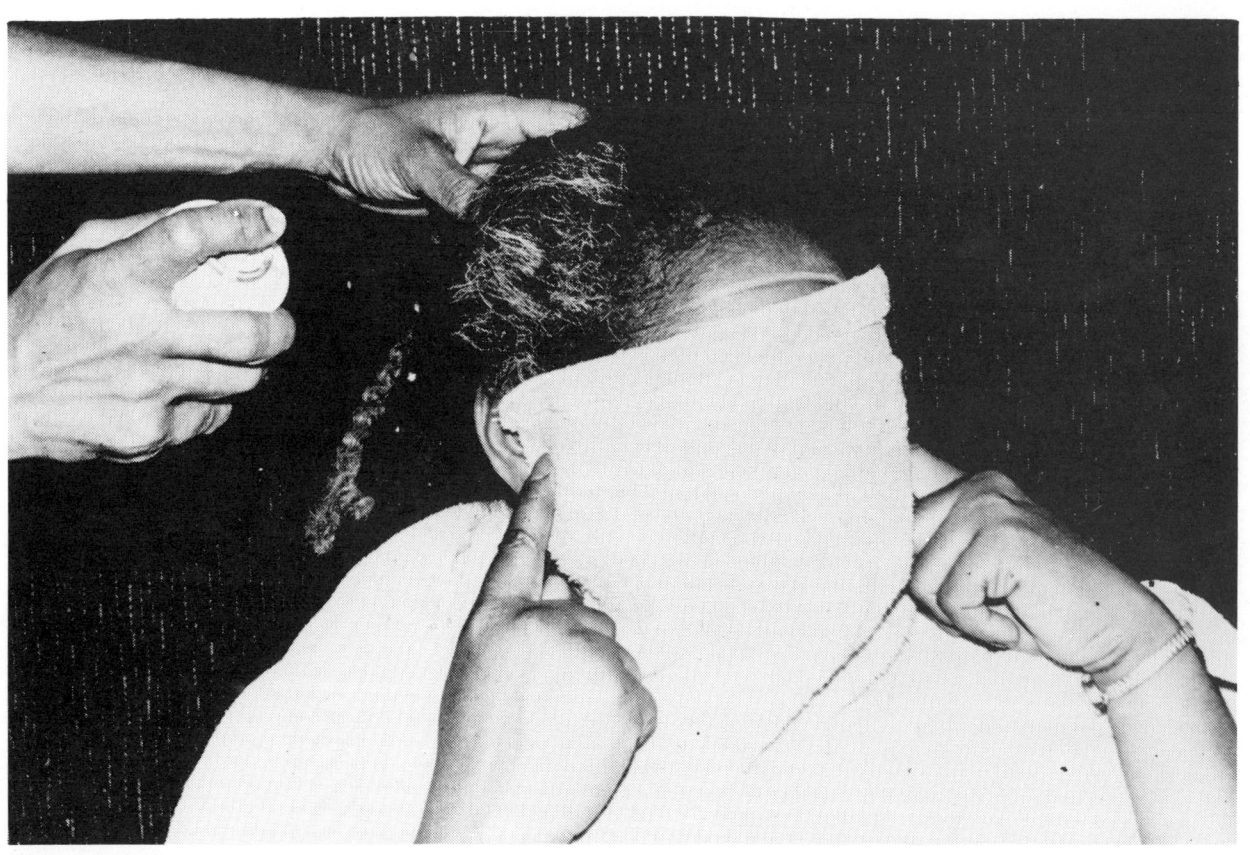

10. The hair is whitened with a spray.

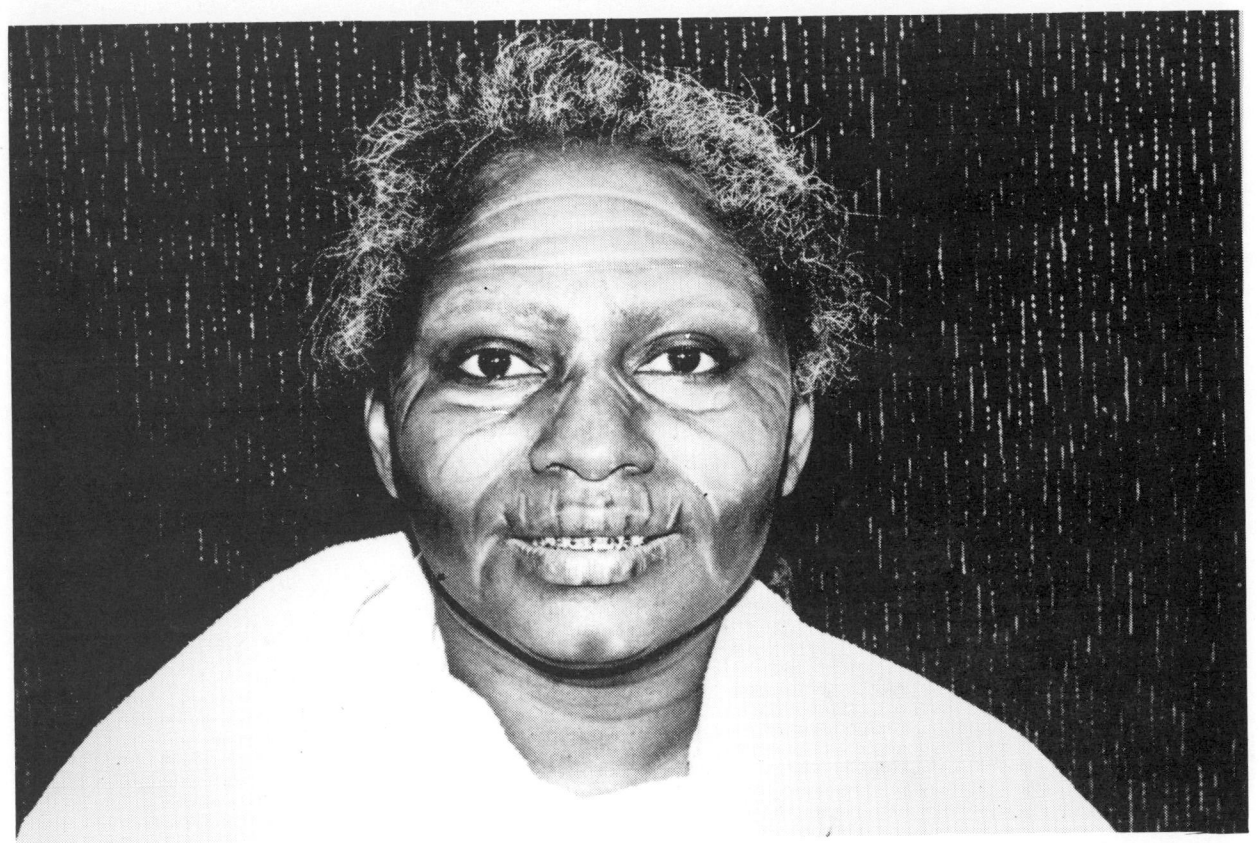

11. The completed makeup for an aged black woman.

Dr. Floyd Sandle agrees with W. K. Waters, Jr., an authority on makeup, that blacks tend to become sallow with age rather than get darker. In order to meet this problem the makeup artist will find that by lightening his base and blending it toward a more olive shade, he will arrive at a fairly suitable old age base tone. The black actor does not tend to age as rapidly where lines are concerned as do many other races. A suggestion is that the makeup artist draw lightly diagonal lines from one side of the face and neck to the other with a dark brown derma pencil. Repeat the process, going in the other direction. The result will be a large number of small, diamond shaped areas which are indistinct from a distance, but which give the feeling of many small age lines. These lines should be drawn after all other makeup has been applied. Powdering will soften them, thus making them sink more effectively into the overall picture.

Highlighting may best be obtained by using a yellow liner (#16 Stein). The purple liner (#21 Stein) is best for low lighting. These must be blended very carefully in order to avoid a grotesque or smudged and dirty appearance.

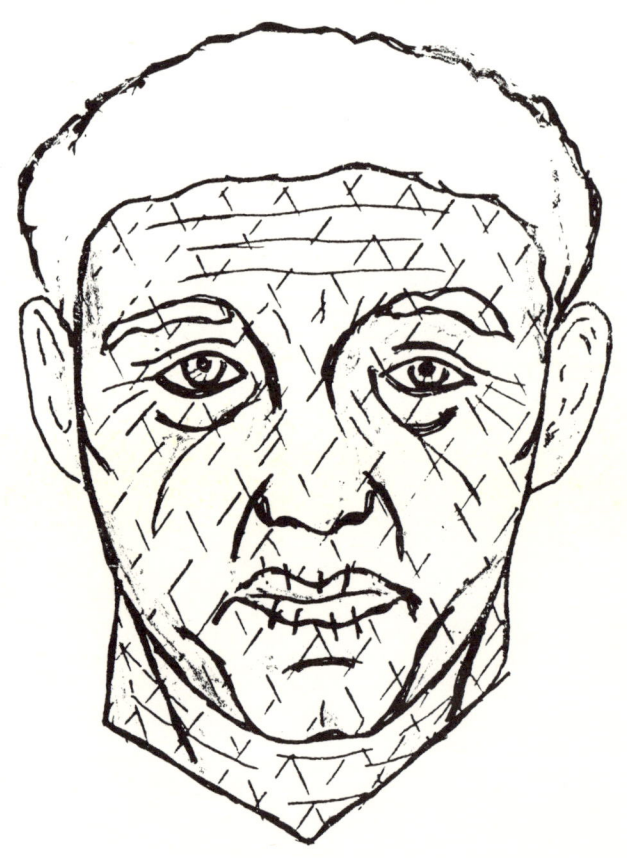

Lightly drawn diagonal lines done with a dark brown pencil to increase the appearance of wrinkles for old age.

Old age makeup for a man

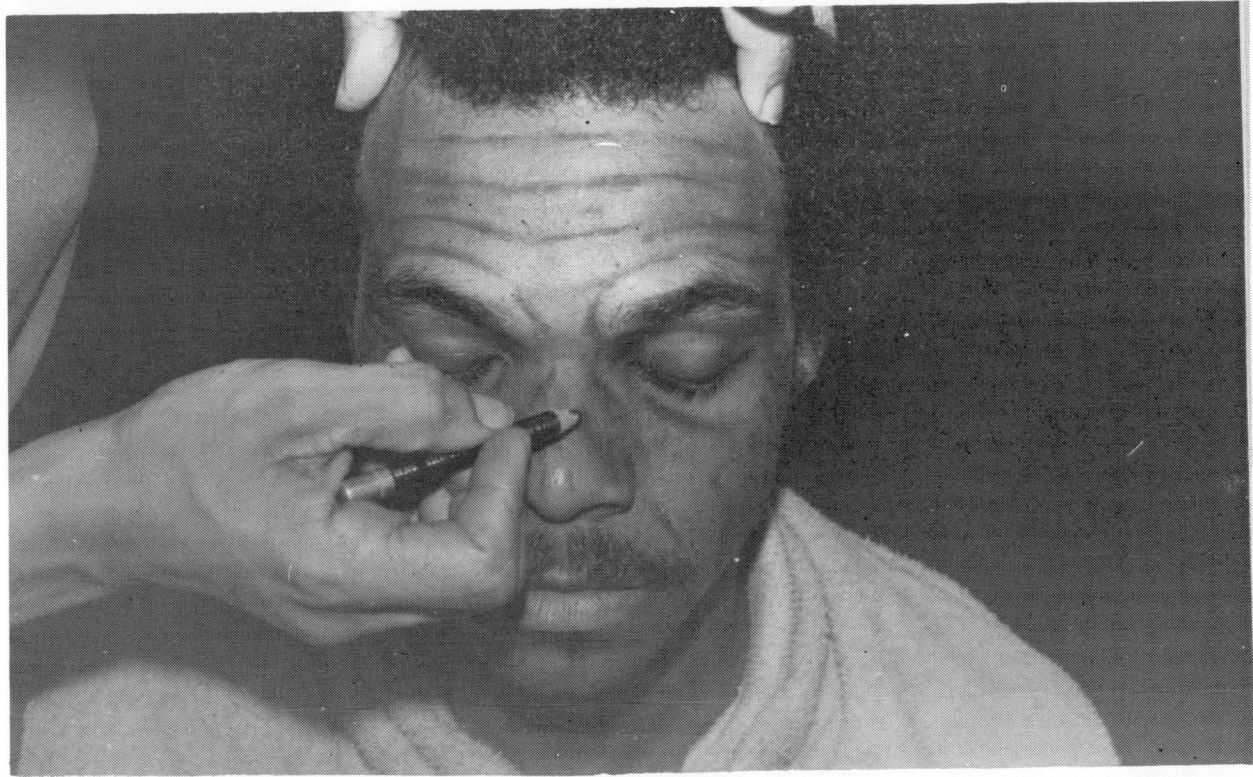

1. After a sallow base, such as Max Factor foundation paint number 5, has been added to the actor's face, lines are placed on the skin to indicate wrinkles. A brown and a yellow liner paint is used.

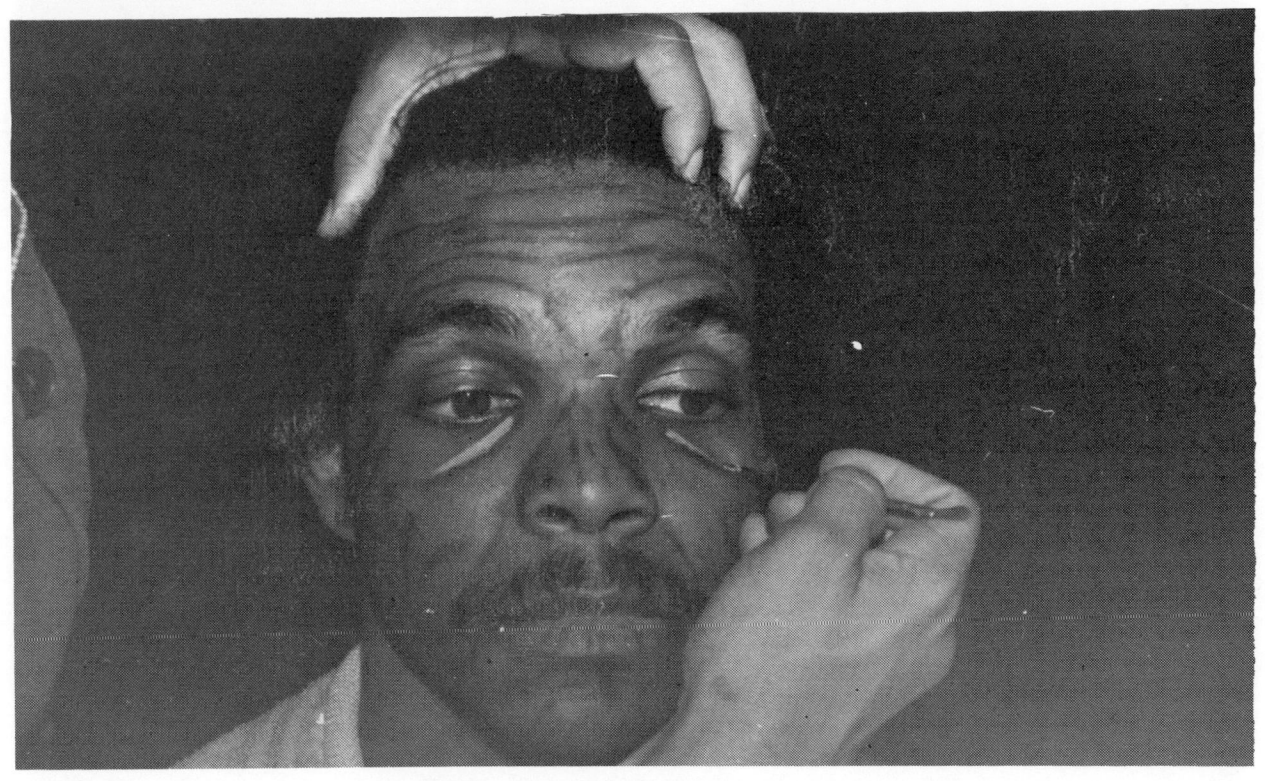

2. Highlights are added to the circles under the eyes.

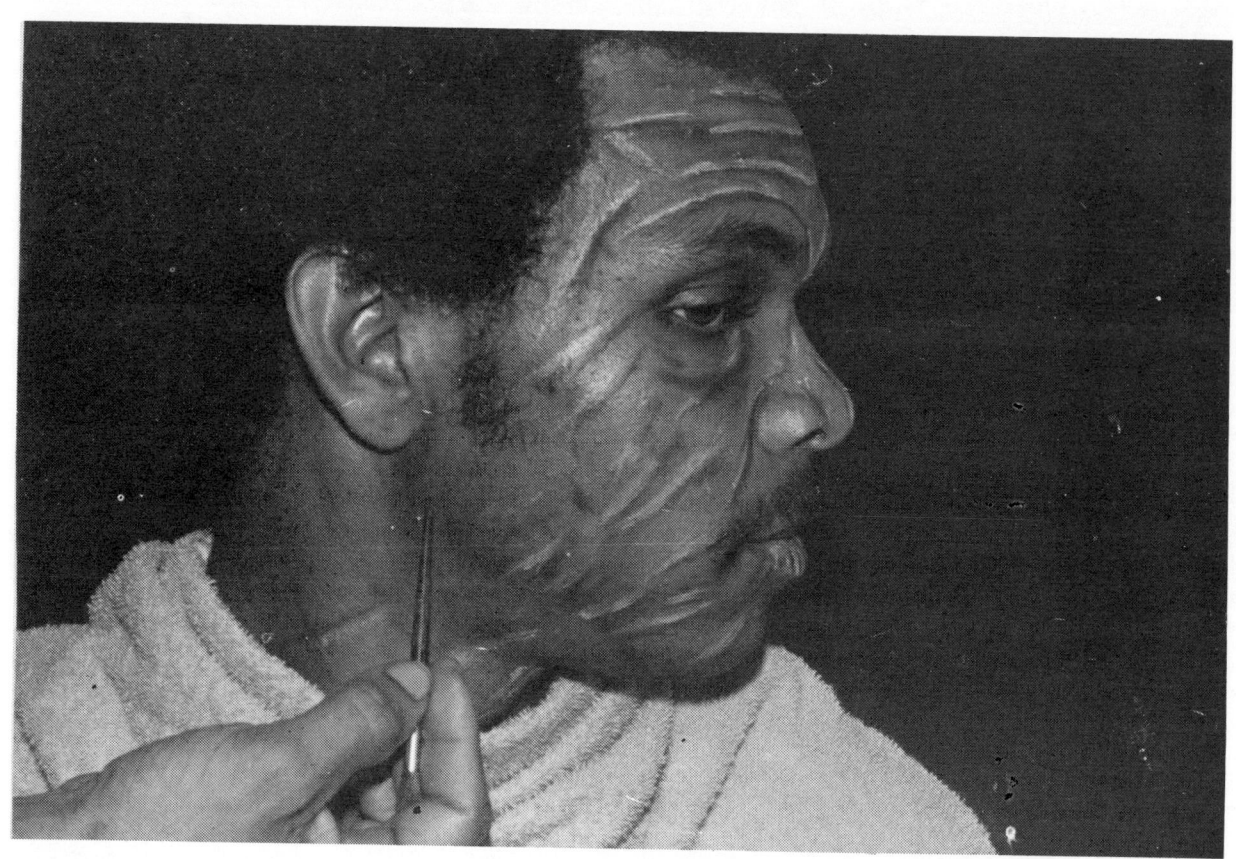

3. Sagging the jowls with dark brown.

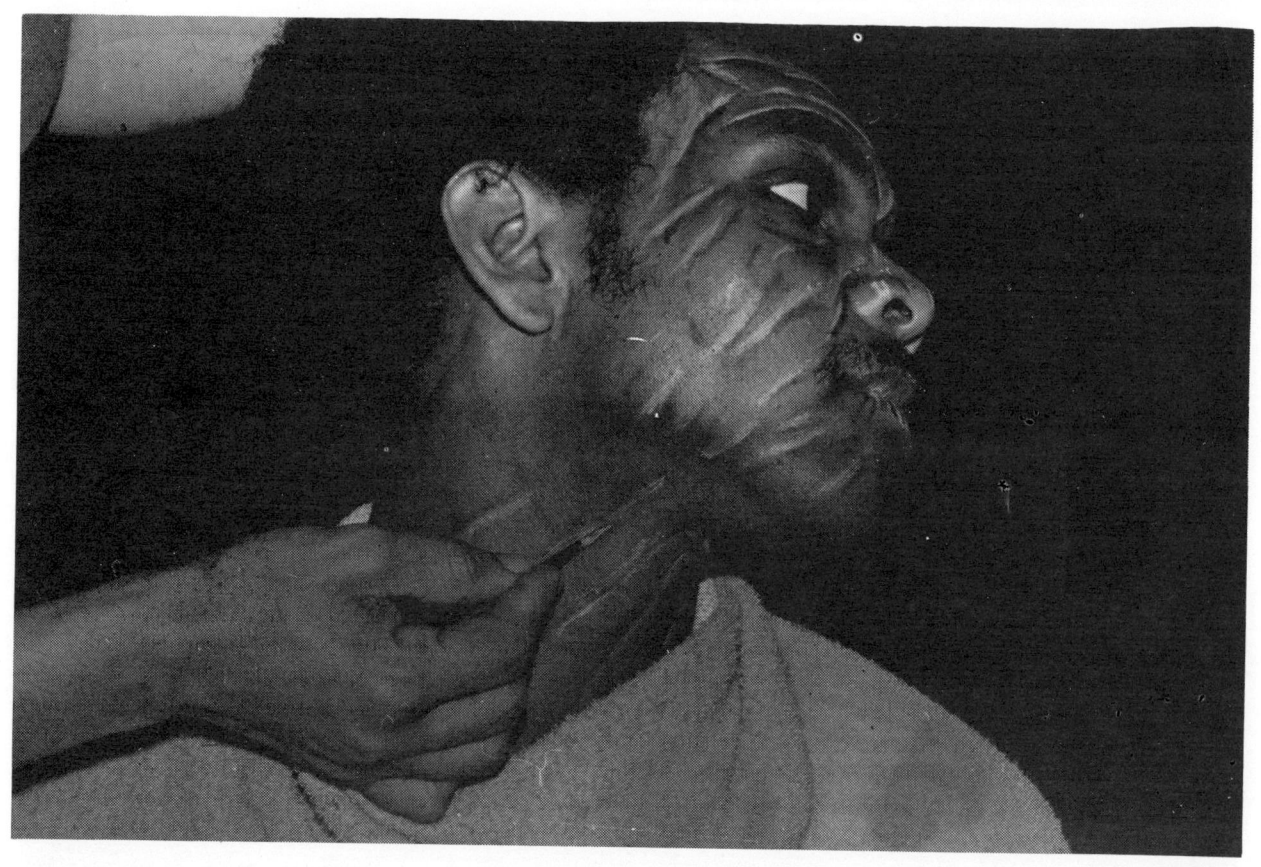

4. Highlighting with a gray liner.

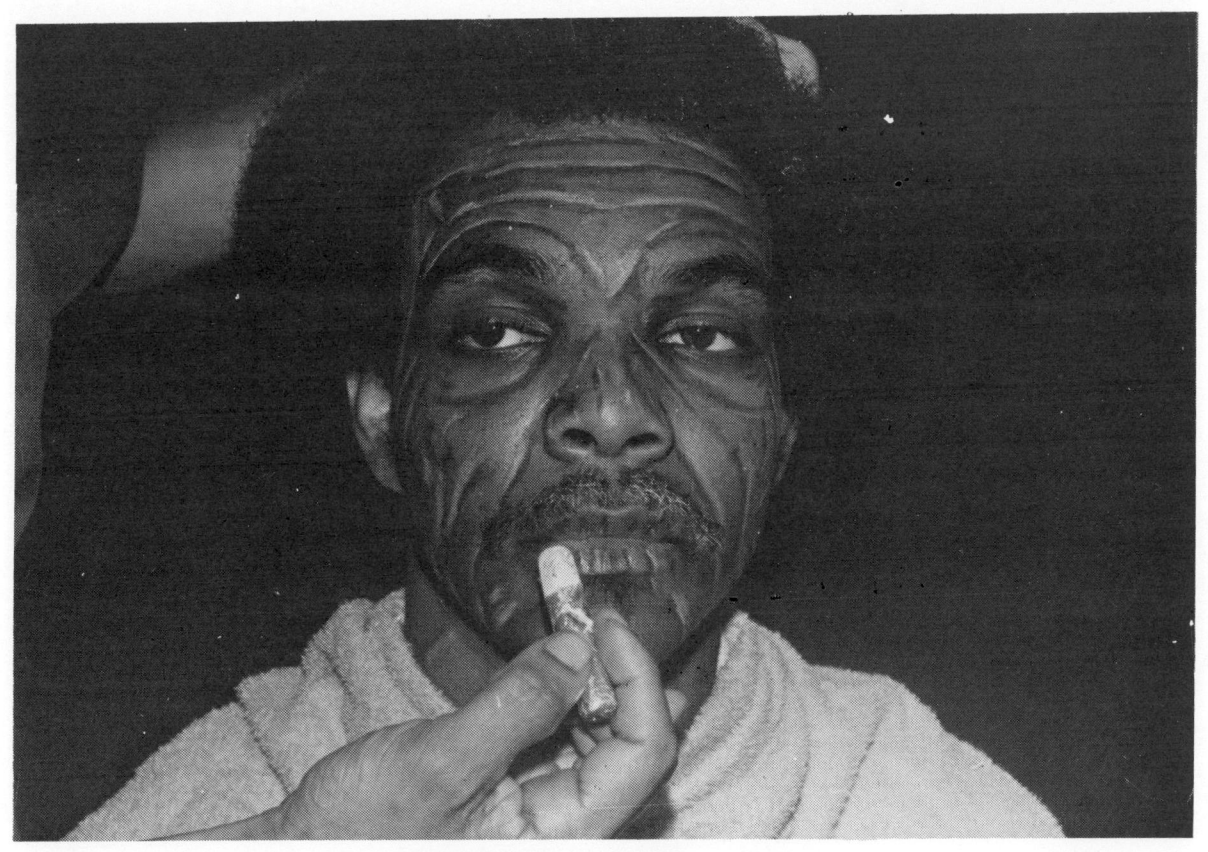

5. Highlighting the lips with a light gray.

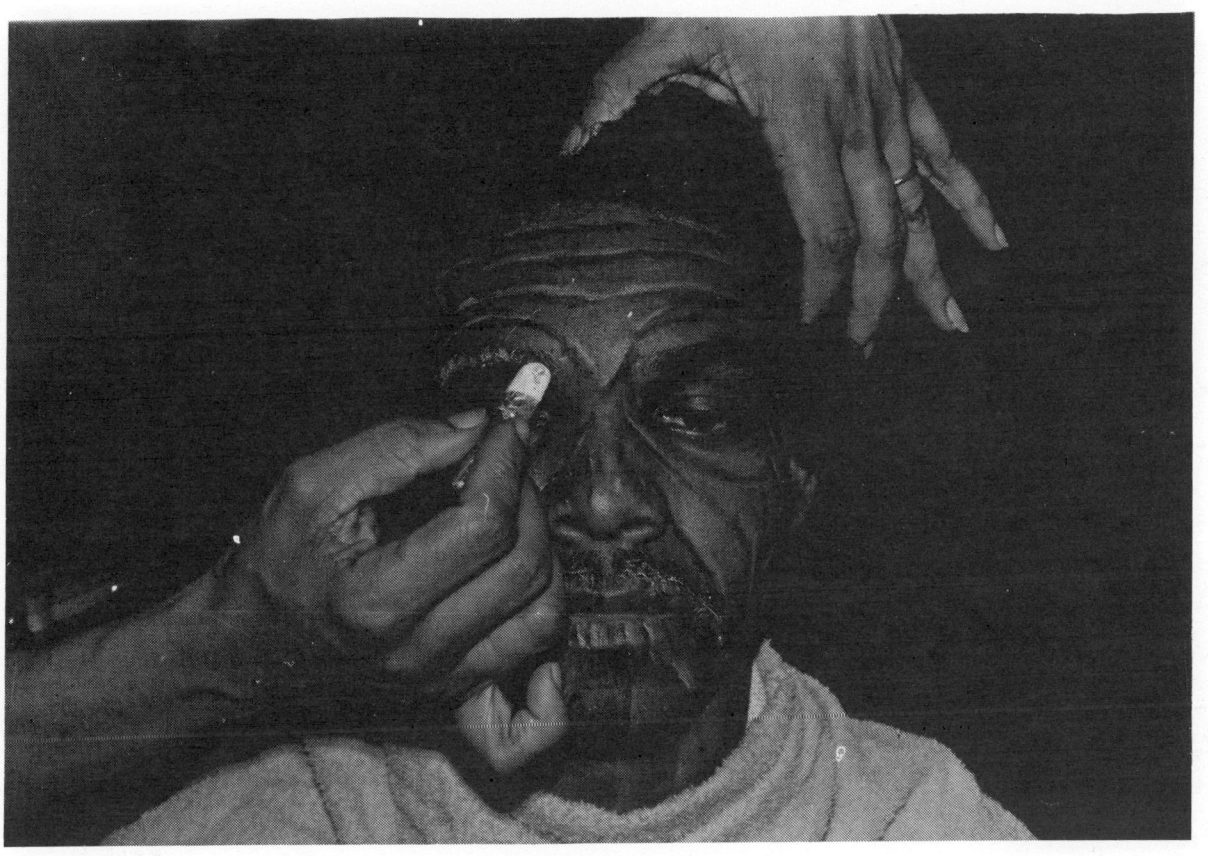

6. Whiting the eyebrows.

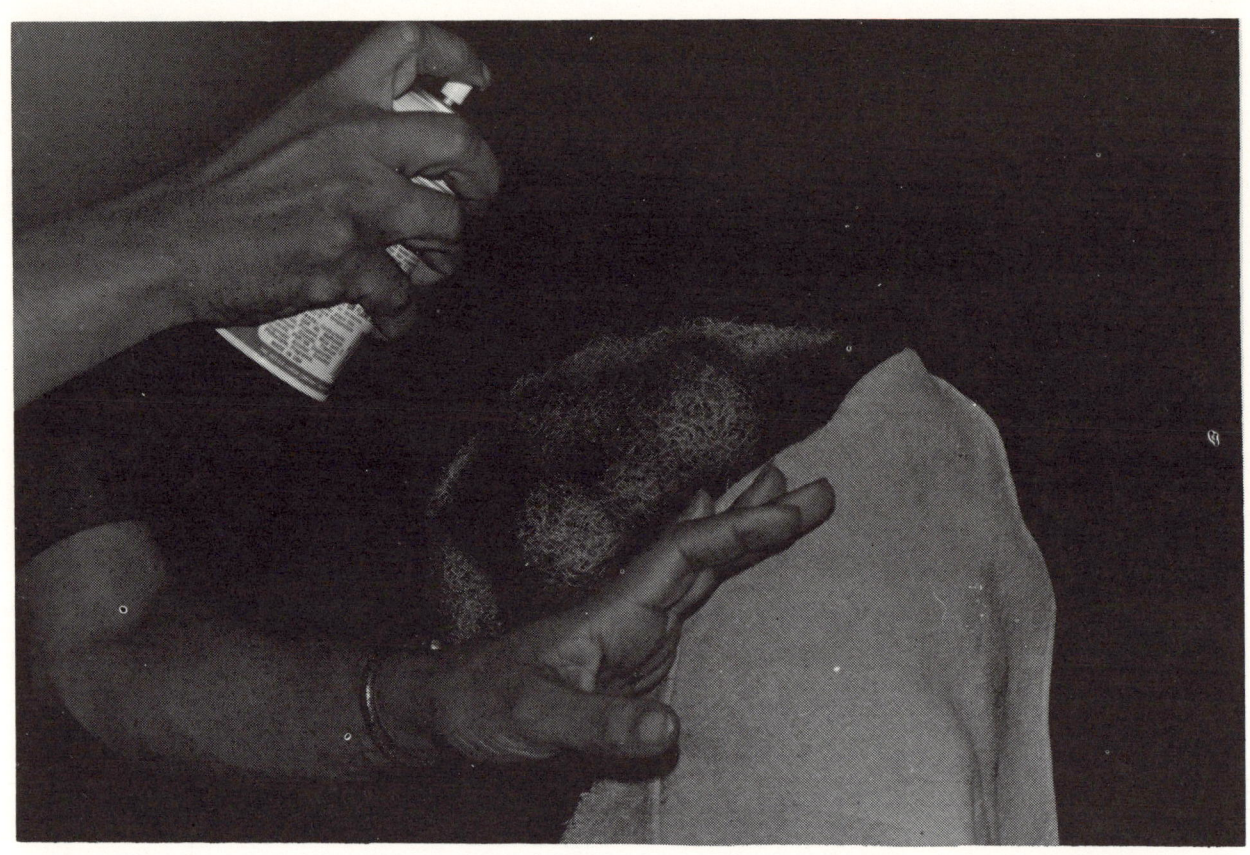

7. Whiting the hair with a white hair spray.

8. Finished old age makeup for male.

For Your Notes

For Your Notes

Chapter V

CHARACTER AND RACIAL MAKEUP

Dark complexioned individuals can make up as races other than their own if their skin is properly colored and their physical features made to appear as those of the people they are to represent.

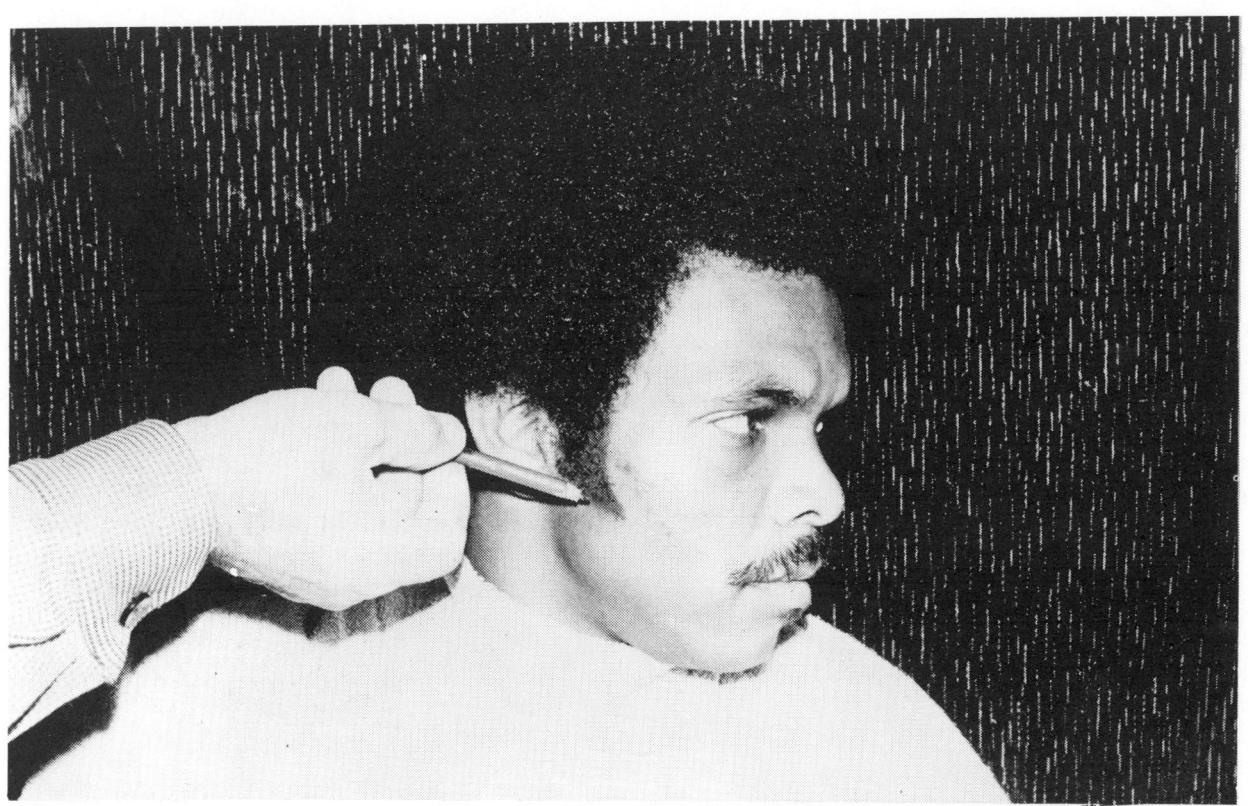

1. Shakespearean Character makeup Iago in *Othello*. Penciling in the hairline with a black derma pencil. This could also be done with the addition of crepe hair and spirit gum.

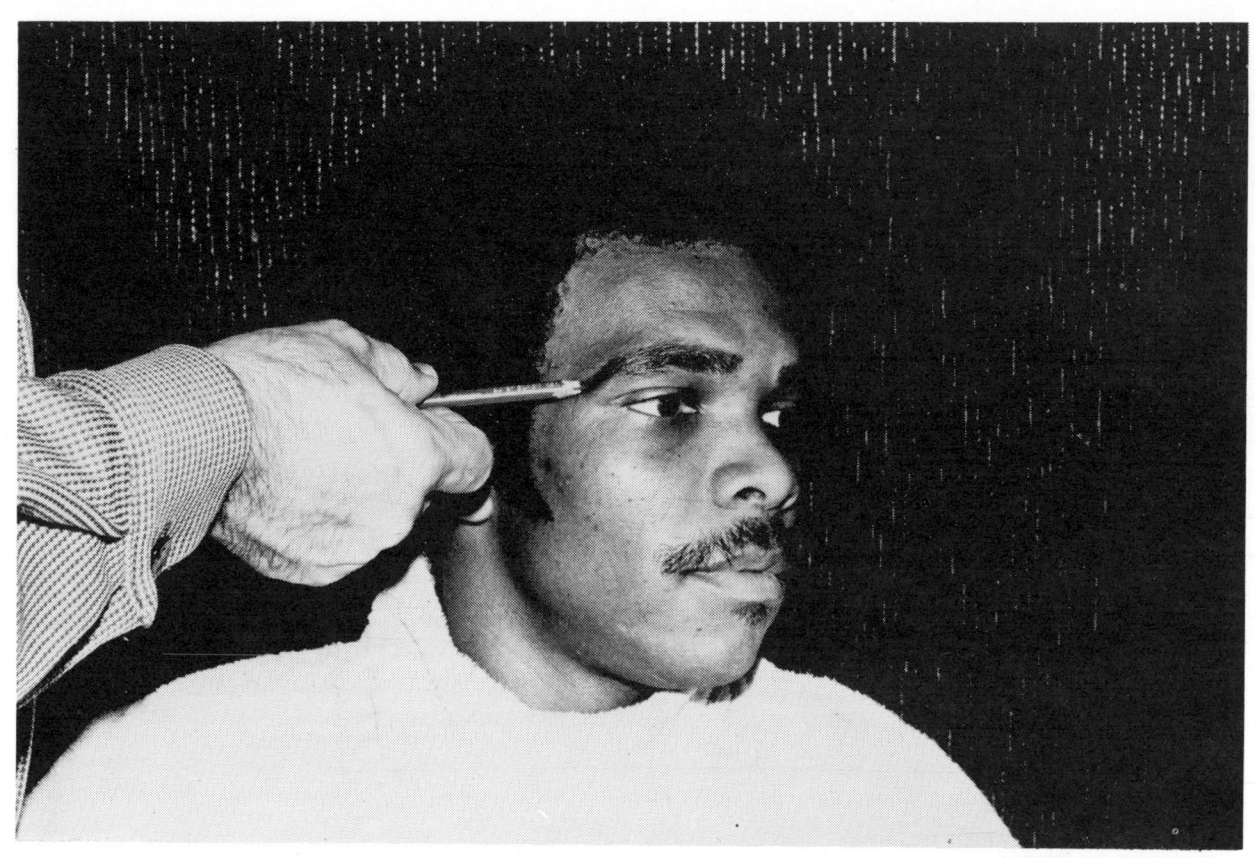

2. Lining the eyebrows.

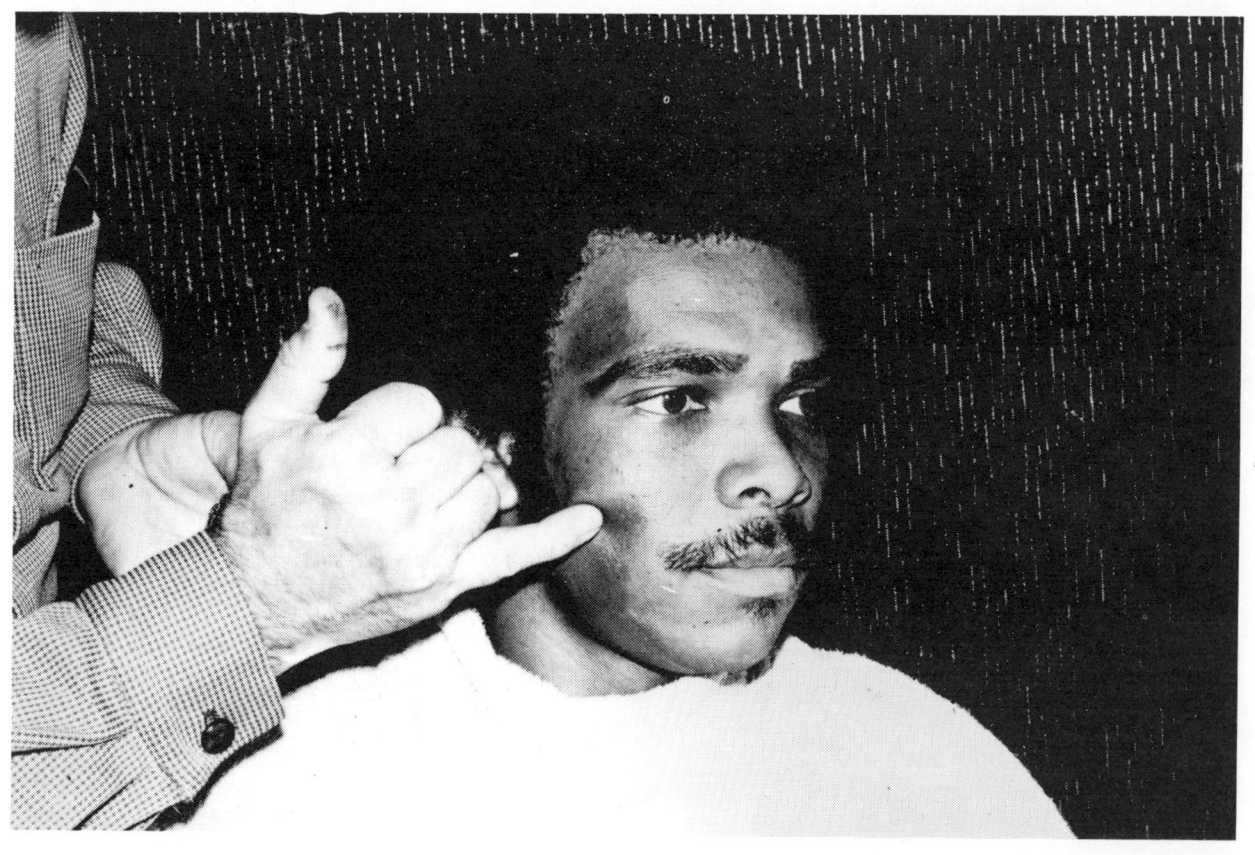

3. Lowlighting the face and neck with brown.

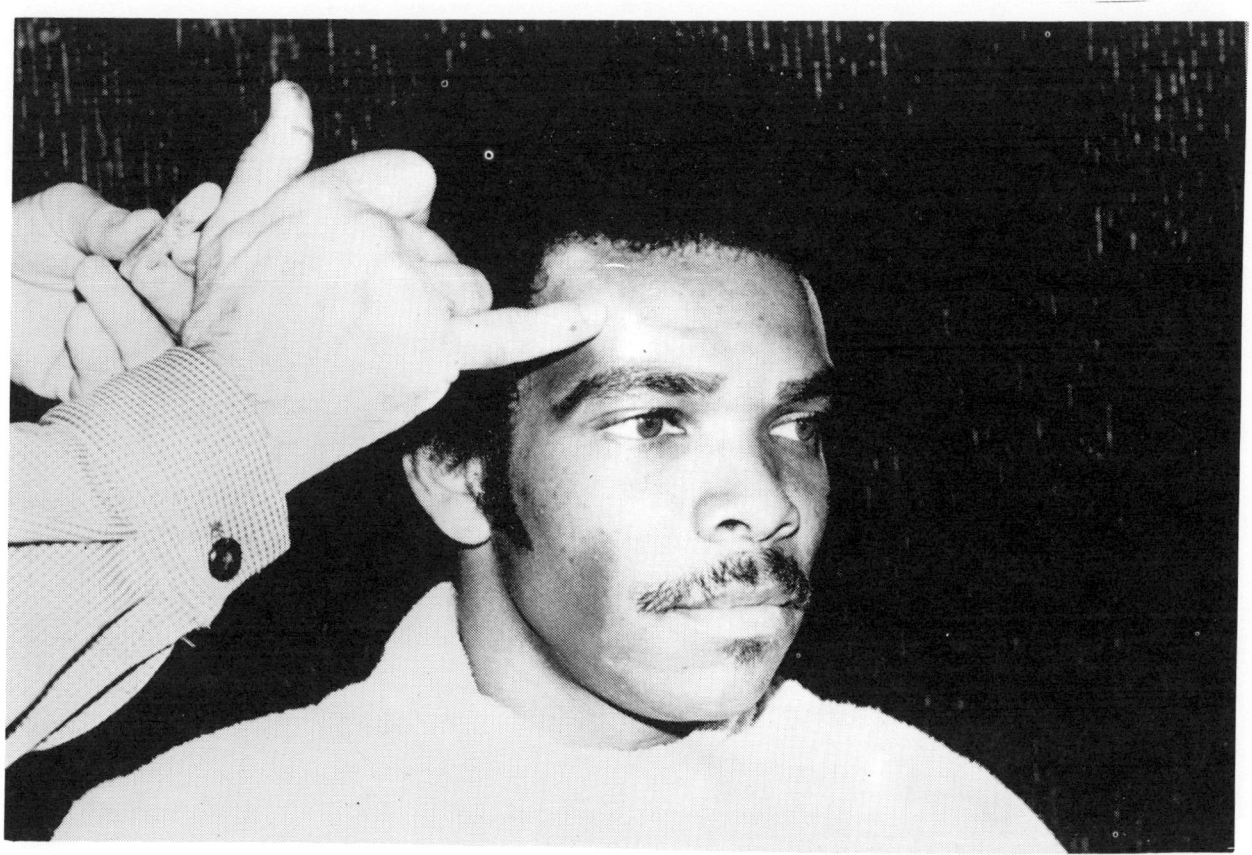

4. Highlighting the forehead in a light tan color. The cheekbones and the neck will also be highlighted.

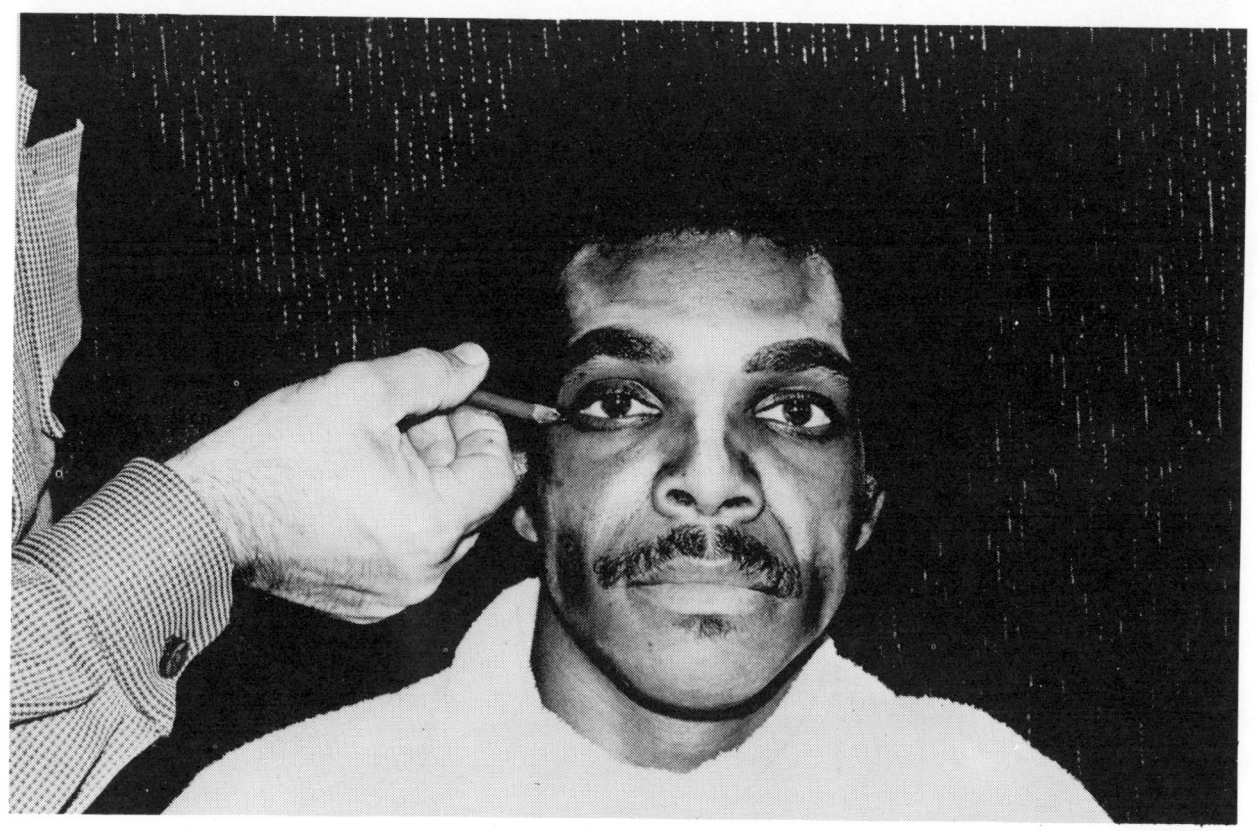

5. Outlining the eyes. Note the highlights and lowlights on the nose.

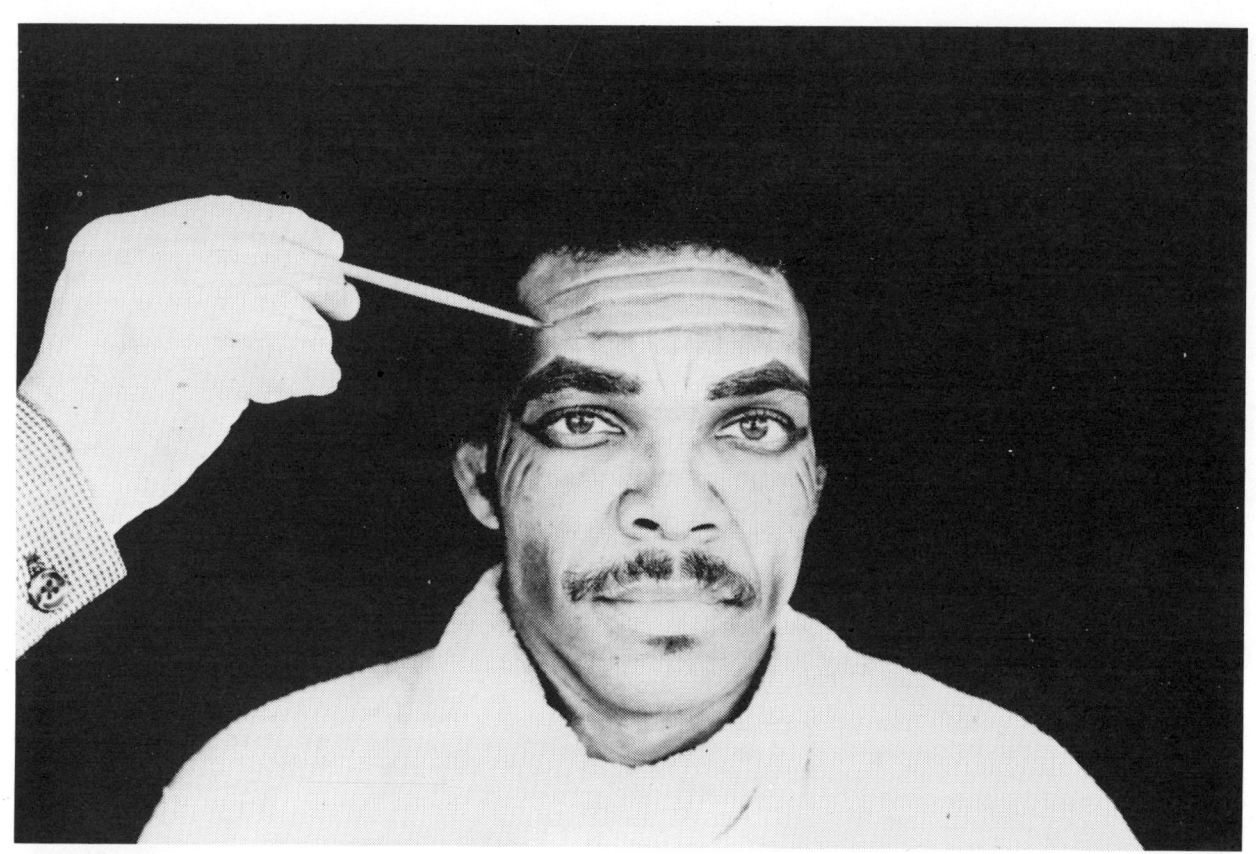
6. Lines are highlighted with a brush and yellow paint.

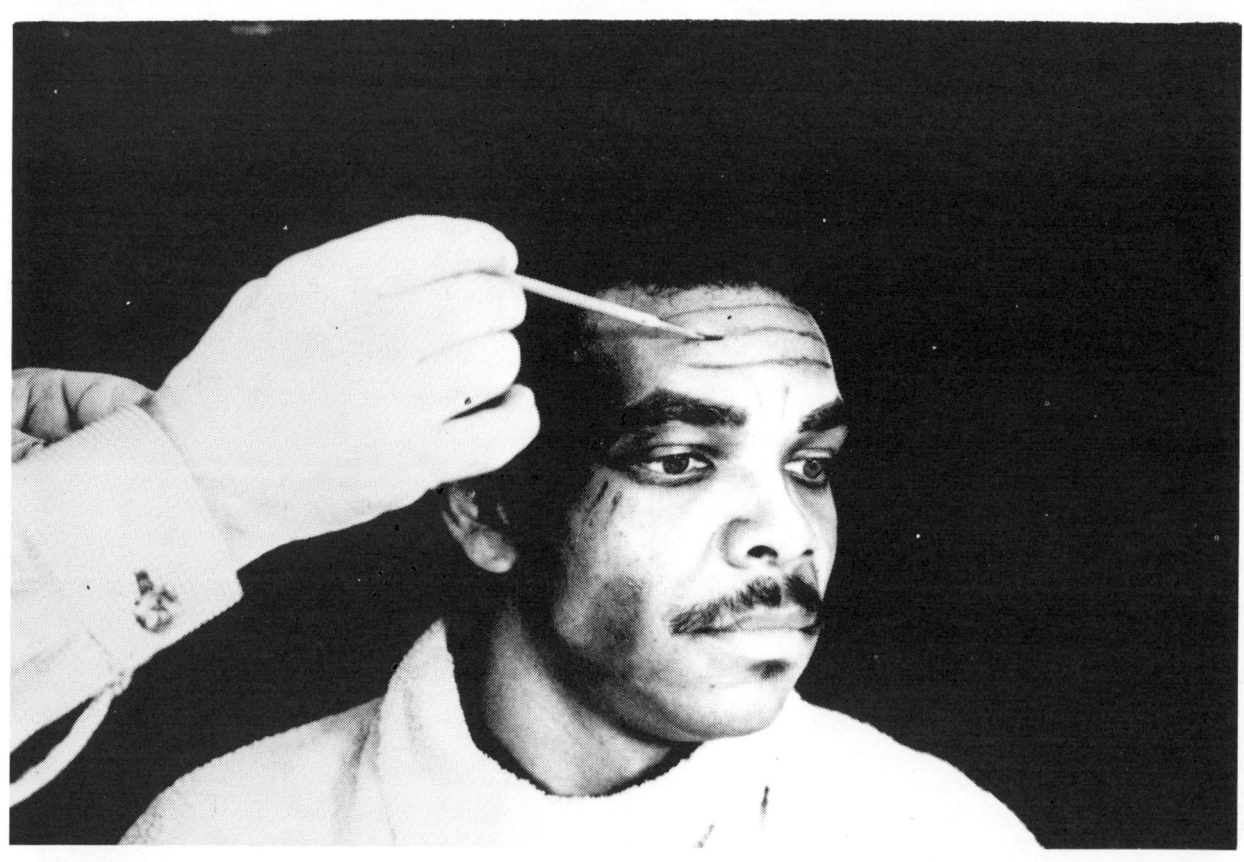
7. Lines are made with a brush and dark brown paint.

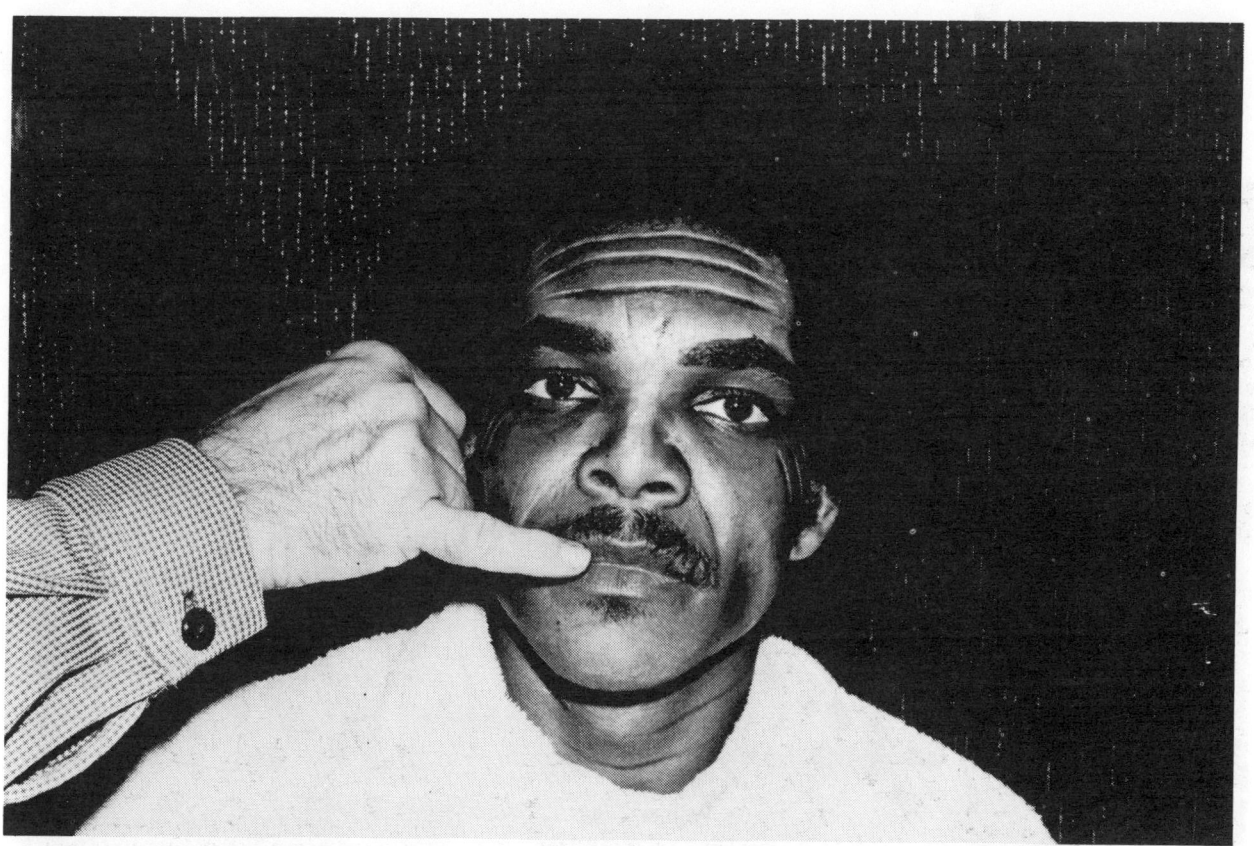

8. Reddish brown lip rouge follows the contours of the natural lips.

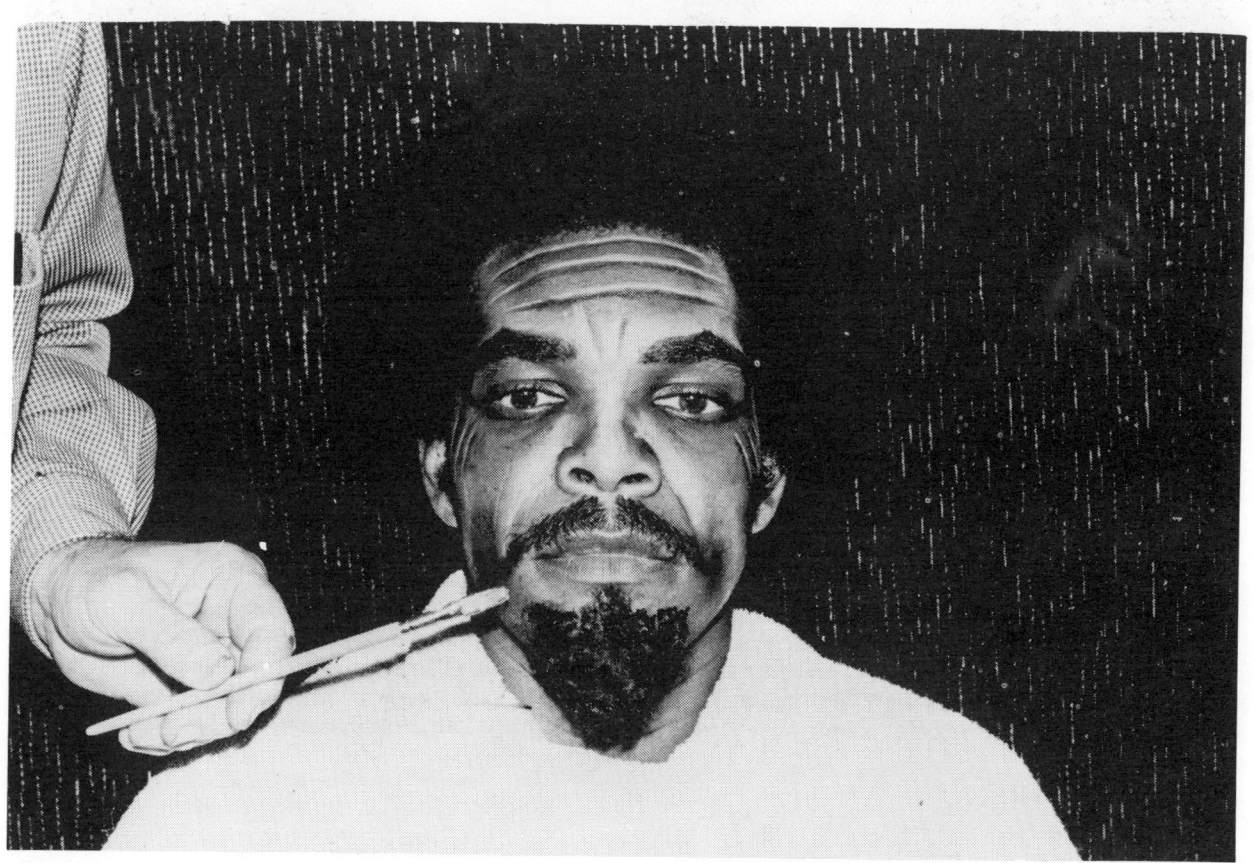

9. The finished makeup with a crepe hair Van Dyke beard.

Character makeup for a Geisha girl. Max Factor's grease paint Number 12 has been used as a foundation base. The model's naturally brown skin tone helps to reduce the strong yellow color in the paint. Remember that many orientals have long fingernails. Artificial nails work well. Males are usually a little more brown than females. Do not use pure yellow or orientals. Oriental eyes appear to slant upwards toward the outer edge of the eyebrows. In order to achieve this effect, a lighter shade of liner or a white base mixed with Max Factor #12 grease paint will highlight the outer lids and give the fleshy appearance which causes the oriental eye to look slanted. The oriental people have straight or wavy black hair, full lips, and round faces.

Procedure for White Makeup on a Black man

Use a grease paint base such as Max Factor #5A. Dot the makeup on all over the face and neck. Blend it smoothly until it covers the desired surfaces including the ears and lips. Go as close to the eyes as safety permits.

To highlight the nose ridge use a lighter color (not white) of grease paint.

For lowlighting the sides of the nose use a darker brown tone on each side of the bridge. This with

A black man made up as a white male

Note the thinned lips, the sharp nose, and the straight hair wig. The mustache and the eyebrows have been lightened to match the color of the wig. Max Factor Number 5A has been used for the foundation paint.

the highlight gives the nose a sharp appearance.
  Line the eyes with brown liner.
  Use brownish red for cheeks and lips. Keep the lips thin.
  Use a straight or curly wig.
  Don't forget to do the hands and feet if they are seen.

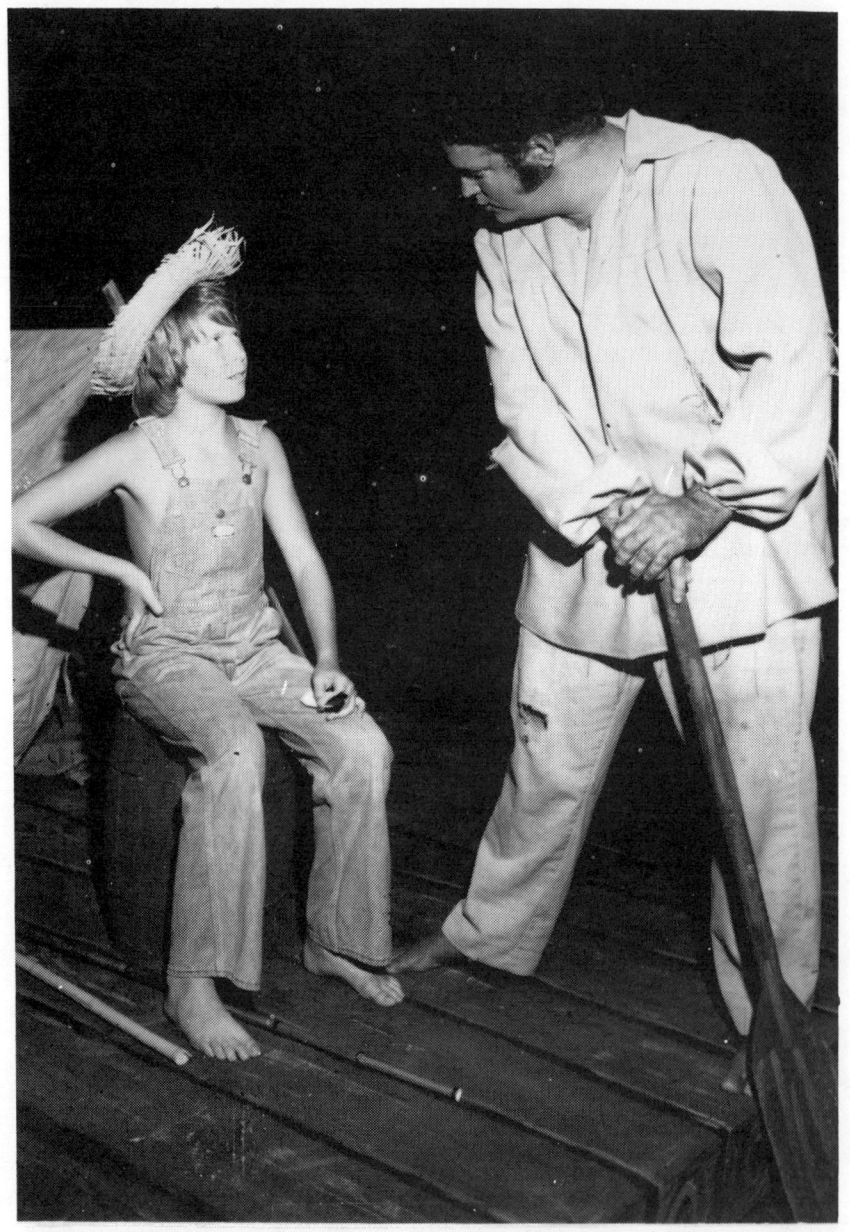

A Caucasian male playing the role of a black man. Notice the makeup on the hands and feet. From the Archives and Special Collection of Northeast Louisiana University.

A black male made up as a Latin type

This is the same male model who appears in the straight makeup picture. Note the curly dark brown wig. Max Factor foundation paint number 6A was used.

Grambling State University actors made up as characters in *The Wizard of Oz*.

Grambling State University *The Wizard of Oz.*

For Your Notes

GLOSSARY

1. **Abolene** is a hypoallergenic cold cream which has a liquid like property and has little or no perfume added. Thus, the hyperallergenic person can use this cleansing agent.
2. **Aquacreme** is a water soluble cold creme that emulsifies grease paint, eliminating the need for tissue or soap.*
3. **Allercreme** is available in a creme or lotion form and contains non-allergic reaction substances. It is recommended for the sensitive or oily skinned person.
4. **Black Eye Paint.** Another name for this product is blemish cover. It is used to cover bruised eyes or skin discolorations. (It is **not** used to give the appearance of a black eye.)*
5. **Black face make-up** is a water soluble make-up which is easily applied and comes in colors including pure black, light or dark negro, Indian, and Hawaiian. Light shades are better for women.
6. **Black tooth wax** is a black wax placed on the teeth to give the appearance of a whole or partial tooth missing. And it is sometimes used to shorten teeth.
7. **Blemi-creme** is a creme preparation (Stein) especially made for covering distractions or undesirable markings on the body such as freckles, acne scars, severely porous skin, and to minimize circles under the eyes.
8. **Brushes** are primarily used in shading the eyes, and painting on lipsticks and for blushing the cheek bones. They are available in various sizes (lengths and widths) to facilitate or accommodate regular or special make-up applications from drawing fine lines to shading lips and eyes. The most common types of brushes are available in sable, camel, or oxhair. Sable is the preferred type.
9. **Cleansing cream** is a theatrical creme used for removing straight make-up and stage make-up and to cleanse the skin.
10. **Crisco** is a vegetable shortening or oil which can be effectively used as make-up remover. One might note it is greaseless and fairly inexpensive. In many instances it can be a substitute for cold cream.
11. **Clown white** is merely white grease paint used primarily for "clown make-up," as its name suggests and can be used as a base coat in preparation for making darker skins lighter when blended with grease paint of a desired color. It also comes in cream form.
12. **Collodion, non-flexible,** is used on scars and crows feet; it contracts the skin as it dries. Flexible is used for building up parts of the face and neck. Some use it instead of spirit gum. (Highly inflammable)*
13. **Color spray** is an aerosol mist intended for temporary color changes to the natural hair, crepe hair and wigs. It can be removed by shampooing.
14. **Crepe hair** is primarily used for male characterizations. Through the application of Latex or spirit gum it can be attached to the skin to form beards, moustaches, side burns, goatee and any other hair applications. It is available in tan, brown, black, and gray.
15. **Derma wax** is sometimes referred to as mortician's wax. It is extremely useful in filling in or raising facial structures. It is not suggested for extension of appendages as in noses and chins because it is too soft and cannot stand firm on its own. It must be mixed with nose putty for strength to hold properly.

16. **Eye lashes** are mounted on strips made of real hair or nylon. They are used when long and heavy lashes are needed or when natural ones are inadequate.* They are easily applied with eyelash adhesive.
17. **Eye shadow** is a creamy substance used to accentuate the eyes to make them larger, smaller, or deeper. Eye shadows come in many different colors and are easily smoothed on with a brush or a stroke of the finger tips.
18. **Eyeliner pencils** are sometimes called Derma pencils (due to their wax-like property) or eye shading pencils (used to outline and shade in the eyebrows.) They are generally used to line or outline facial structures.
19. **Face powder** is patted with a powder puff on or over greasepaints to prevent smudging and smearing of the makeup. It sets the makeup.
20. **Face powder brushes** are great for powders to the face and blushes to the cheeks leaving a velvety effect. They are a supple nylon or real hair.
21. **Fostril** is a medicated drying lotion that is flesh tinted and greaseless. It contains sulphur along with a drying agent. It is translucent, hypoallergenic and can be used as a base for theatrical make-up. (It is used in the treatment of acne.)
22. **Grease paint** is a stick or soft grease in Stein, and soft only in Factor and Mehron. Most commonly used foundation to give the basic skin coloring. Apply in dot or criss-cross form, then fill in the area in circular fashion. Use only enough to tint the skin. Be sure to specify: (1) Brand, (2) Stick or Soft. The numbers on each brand and type of makeup do not match each other.*
23. **Hair whitener** is bottled as a liquid and is used to gray the hair by using a toothbrush or the finger tips.
24. **Hyperallergic skin** has a low tolerance for non-medicated products and is susceptible to allergic reactions; for example, developing rashes and skin discolorations. The person who has such a condition should use hypoallergenic makeup and cleansing cream.
25. **Hypoallergic skin** can tolerate the use of regular makeup and removing creams. Usually this is normal skin, not too oily or too dry.
26. **Liners or Lining colors** – in soft and stick form. Used for highlights and shadows.*
27. **Lip liners** – used merely to outline or define the lips. One may choose a wooden pencil or an automatic pencil.
28. **Liquid latex** comes in tan, white, and flesh. Flesh and tan are used in making beards as well as applying them, since it holds the beards together, allowing the beard to be reused. It should not be applied on the actor's hair. **There is no solvent or remover for solidified Latex.** White latex dries clear and is used for aging the skin. Latex can also be used with amazing results to make false noses, chins, high cheeks, facial distortions, etc. **Latex should not be used on any person who is allergic to make up.***
29. **Liquid make-up** is an aqueous mixture of powder with suspending agents. It dries flat. Apply with a wet sponge. It is recommended where large areas are to be covered, and, thus, is good for chorus work in musicals. We estimate 1½ oz. to 2 oz. per person for complete body coverage as an average figure.*
30. **Luminescent Products** are used to produce spectacular color and lighting effects in darkened surroundings. They do not contain radium, phosphor or other harmful chemicals. Ultra violet light is also harmless and will not affect the eyes or the skin. the make-up is available in cream form and is applied over the regular nose. Stein makes only green (considered the most effective), while Leichner makes yellow and red as well as green. Both make UV as well as phosphorescent make-up. (no UV light is required, but the room must be absolutely dark.)*
31. **Marcelle** is a hypoallergenic make-up remover, prepared for the oily skin and non-oily skin, to remove make-up causing no irritation or damage to the skin.

32. **Moist rouge** is used to add color and a warm glow to the cheek area and, sometimes, to add color to the lips. It can be used to accentuate the cheekbone. Apply to the cheek with the fingertips and to the lips with a brush. It is available in various tints of red, light red to deep dark red.
33. **Nose putty** is a pliable, plastic material that is flesh colored and is used for changing the shape of the nose and other bony parts of the face. Knead a small amount in the palm with lightly cold creamed finger tips and then work into the area. If it's too stiff, soften with a little hot or cold cream. It will adhere with the use of spirit gum and sometimes by itself. Heavy perspiration will require touch-up repairs between scenes.*
34. **Pancake** is a cake make-up in dry form which can be applied with a sponge and water. It is available in various shades and colors.
35. **Panchromatic** make-up was originally discovered for panchromatic film, a film sensitive to all colors, recording them in their true harmonious relations, and eliminating finally those sharp, hard contrasts, so common with the use of the old time orthochromatic film. Since then this make-up has given the performer a standard range of complexion tones that balances, and which can withstand the color absorption properties of every lighting device. The colorings of pancro make-up are neutral tones of tan and warm brown. **Pancro,** thus is a term, not a make-up, and is available as grease paint, face powder, pancake, liquid make-up, and pan stick. There are corresponding pancro shades in liner and moist rouge. The numbering series correspond to each other (22 powder equals 22 grease and 23 grease is one shade darker than 22). No. 21 is a very light pink; 22 is a light pink; 23 is the best female shade, while 24 is a good shade for dark brunettes or light males. No. 26 and 27 are the best male shades; #28 and #31 are for dark males.*
36. **Panstick** is a creamy make-up which is in "stick form." The oily skinned person may prefer this make-up, in that it contains less oil than grease paints. It is available in many shades.
37. **Sealer** by Mehron is a new product. It is a liquid plastic skin adhesive used medically as a protective coating. It is useful in make-up in order to provide a better make-up surface for derma wax construction and for blocking out eye-brows.*
38. **Skincote** is made for the hyperallergic person with sensitive skin. It is a non-oily cream which serves as a protective undercoat especially where metallic make-up or latex is applied to the skin.
39. **Spirit gum** is a strong, colorless liquid adhesive used to apply beards and other artificial hair pieces to the skin. (Crepe hair is used as artificial hair.) Alcohol will remove the spirit gum from the skin.
40. **Texas dirt** is an extraordinarily effective body make-up which comes in powder form. It can be used dry with a wet sponge or mixed with water. It goes on very easily and can be applied quickly. A little goes a long way. For face only, 1 lb. will cover approximately 75 to 100 persons, while for complete body, a pound will cover from 25 to 35 people. It is made by two firms, one in Texas, and the other by Mehron. Mehron makes three different shades: regular—silver—gold. The regular is much redder and the silver and gold have a metallic luster. Regular Texas Dirt has an unusual effect on the skin, making it appear "alive." It originally was discovered by a dance group on tour of Texas.*
41. **Tooth enamel** – Leichner. It is used for concealing gold-filled or discolored teeth. It is easily removed with alcohol or by merely scraping it off. It comes in shades of white, ivory, and pearl grey, and also in black, which is used for blacking out teeth.
42. **Under rouge** – has less intense color than moist rouge, being more on the pink side. It is intended for cheek rouge and shadowing. It is used to subdue prominent cheek bones and double chin. It is also used as lipstick for men.*
43. **Valtex** – a latex which dries clean. It is used for aging or "pulling" the skin.*

---

*William, Allen, *A Theatre Handbook*, Grambling State University (1976) Pages 123, 124, 125, 126, 127.

APPENDIX

Additional information for Black Theatre Makeup, taken from the booklet *Makeup for the Profession,* by M. Stein Cosmetic Co.

The Black performer unlike the Caucasian, can more readily use his own skin tone as a base to start with. But, in view of the achievements in the American theater which has discarded stereotyping a greater range of available performing roles than heretofore, it is possible to alter the skin tone many shades lighter if need be. Once your basic skin color has been determined, either your own or lighter or darker, you can follow the same procedure of make-up techniques as described throughout the booklet.

Your shadows, usually about 3 shades darker than your base can be made up by blending Stein's Lining Colors, #7, 13, and 17 in dealing with the dark skin. But for the lightened skin you will resort to lighter shading colors. Your highlights will naturally be about 3 shades lighter than the base. In order to keep your skin tone from "bleeding" thru the lighter base, use first an undertone of Stein's Blemi-Creame (light, medium or dark) blended in smoothly before proceeding with the lighter base. Generally, it is always advisable to make the dark skin a few shades lighter for better film registration in black and white or color. This is equally true of the Caucasian performer who needs a darker skin tone.

For a base to enhance your natural skin color in stage make-up, use Soft Paint – 7F, 9, 10, 16, 19 or 20 and match the respective color in Stein's Face Powder or use 1A Neutral (colorless). If your stage role can hold the make-up for the entire performance with little perspiration, you can also use Velvet Stick or Cake Make-up – 7, 9, 32, 38, 39, 51 or 52. In selecting Cake Make-up use one shade lighter than corresponding Velvet Stick because it has more opacity. The female performer will naturally use the lighter shades of the above suggested bases.

An Individual Makeup Chart

Play _____

Character _____ Actor's Name _____

Age

Racial or
Ethnic _____

State of
Health _____
_____

Special Requirements
of script _____
_____

Make-Up Materials
Foundation _____
Rouge _____
Eyeliners _____
Liners for modeling
Highlight _____
Shadow _____
Eyelashes _____
Eyebrows _____
Powder _____
Body Make-Up _____
Hair Items _____
_____
Special Effects _____
_____

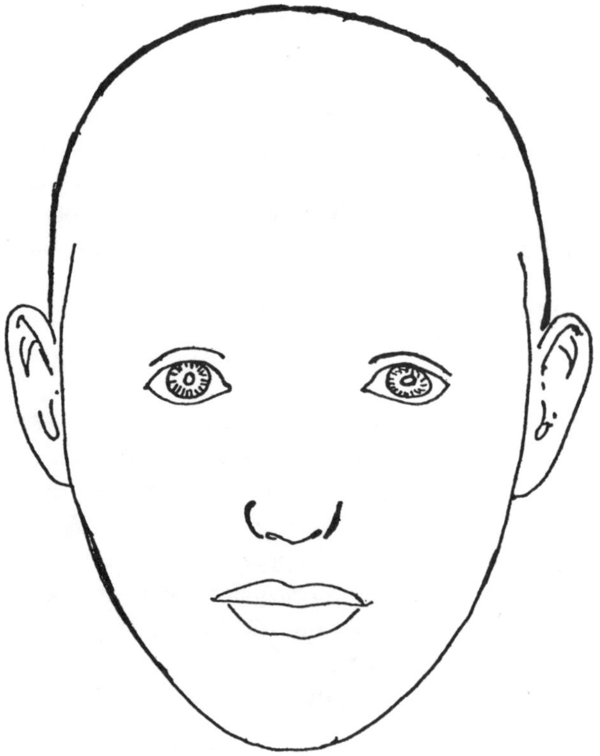

From *A Theatre Handbook* by Allen Williams, Grambling State University (1976) p.128.

Plays for Predominately Black Characters by title, author, and publisher

Amen Corner, James Baldwin, Samuel French, Inc.
Anna Lucasta, Philip Yordan, Dramatists Play Service, Inc.
Big Time Buck White, Joseph Dolan Tuotti, Samuel French, Inc.
Blacks, The, Jean Genet, Samuel French, Inc.
Blues For Mr. Charlie, James Balwin, Baker's Plays.
Ceremonies In Dark Old Men, Lonnie Elder III, Baker's Plays.
For Colored Girls Who Have Considered Suicide When The Rainbow Is Enough, Ntozaki Shange, Samuel French, Inc.
Green Pastures, Marc Connelly, Dramatists Play Service, Inc.
In Abraham's Bosom, Paul Green, Samuel French, Inc.
Les Blanc, Lorraine Hansberry, Samuel French, Inc.
Mean To Be Free, Joanna Kraus, New Plays For Children.
Native Son, Paul Green and Richard Wright, Samuel French, Inc.
No Place To Be Somebody, Charles Gordone, Samuel French, Inc.
Ododo (Musical), Joseph A. Walker, Samuel French, Inc.
Purlie (Musical), Ossie Davis, Phillip Rose, Peter Udell, music by Gary Geld, Samuel French, Inc.
Purlie Victorious, Ossie Davis, Baker's Plays.
Raisin (Musical), Lorraine Hansberry, Robert Nemiroff, Charlotte Zaltzberg, music by Judd Woldin, lyrics by Robert Brittan, Samuel French, Inc.
Raisin In The Sun, Lorraine Hansberry, Baker's Plays.
Sign In Sidney Brustein's Window, Lorraine Hansberry, Samuel French, Inc.
Treemonisha (Folk Opera), Scott Joplin, Dramatic Publishing Co.
To Be Young Gifted and Black, Lorraine Hansberry, Samuel French, Inc.
Wiz, The (Musical), L. Frank Baumand, William Brown (music and lyrics) Charlie Smalls, Samuel French, Inc.

MAKEUP COMPANIES

At present there is no company that is in the business of producing black makeup for the stage. Most of the standard theatrical makeup companies, such as Stein, Max Factor and Ben Nye, manufacture a fine variety of basic shades ranging from a very light pink to a very dark brown. They have everything that is needed to create a great looking character. By judicious mixing, the makeup artist can usually arrive at a satisfactory base for his actors when it is needed. The most successful shades for such mixing are Stein's soft grease paints #4, #14 and #20. Using #14 as a dominant tone, one can lighten or darken it with #4 or #20 respectively in cases where less pink or redness is desired. Number 16 may be substituted for #20, but it should be carefully checked under the stage lights, for it tends to give a rather deep red tinge to the complexion. A word of caution: avoid making the base color too light: it could look like a death mask.

A large number of makeup houses such as Fashion Fair, Flori Roberts, Ambi, Johnson's Products and several others, specialize in makeup for fashionable black women. Many of these products are more than adequate for general theatrical makeup.

Perhaps Stein, Max Factor and Ben Nye make the most practical makeup for the black actor.

ADDRESSES OF MAJOR DISTRIBUTORS OF MAKEUP

1. Bob Kelly
   151 West 46th Street
   New York, NY 10036

2. Ben Nye, Inc.
   11571 Santa Monica Blvd.
   Los Angeles, California 90025
   (213) 478-1558

3. Fashion Fair Cosmetics
   820 South Michigan St.
   Chicago, Ill. 60605

4. Leichner Creative Studio
   44A Cranbaum Street, London
   W.C. 2, England

5. M. Stein Cosmetic Co.
   430 Broome Street
   New York City, NY 10013

6. Max Factor, Co.
   P.O. Box 2323
   Hollywood, California 90028
   (213) 462-6131

7. Mehron, Inc.
   250 W. 40th Street
   New York, NY 10018
   (212) 997-1011